First World War
and Army of Occupation
War Diary
France, Belgium and Germany

18 DIVISION
Divisional Troops
79 Field Company Royal Engineers
25 July 1915 - 30 April 1919

WO95/2027/1

The Naval & Military Press Ltd
www.nmarchive.com
Published in association with The National Archives

Published by

The Naval & Military Press Ltd

Unit 10 Ridgewood Industrial Park,

Uckfield, East Sussex,

TN22 5QE England

Tel: +44 (0) 1825 749494

www.naval-military-press.com

www.nmarchive.com

This diary has been reprinted in facsimile from the original. Any imperfections are inevitably reproduced and the quality may fall short of modern type and cartographic standards.

© **Crown Copyright**
Images reproduced by permission of The National Archives, London, England, 2015.

Contents

Document type	Place/Title	Date From	Date To
Heading	WO95/2027/1		
Heading	18th Division 79th Field Coy R.E. Jly 1915-Mar 1919		
Heading	18th Division 79th F.C.R.E Vol I from 25th To 31st July 1915		
Heading	18th Division 79th F.C.R.E. Vol II from 31.8.15		
Miscellaneous	49th Fed Coy Rt	01/09/1915	01/09/1915
War Diary	Codford	25/07/1915	25/07/1915
War Diary	Southampton	26/07/1915	26/07/1915
War Diary	Havre	27/07/1915	27/07/1915
War Diary	Longueau	28/07/1915	28/07/1915
War Diary	Septenville	28/07/1915	31/07/1915
War Diary	Septenville & Millencourt	01/08/1915	03/08/1915
War Diary	Aveluy	04/08/1915	17/08/1915
War Diary	Laneuville Les Bray	18/08/1915	20/08/1915
War Diary	Bray	21/08/1915	31/08/1915
Heading	18th Division 79th F.C.R.E. Vol 3 Sept 15		
War Diary	Bray	01/09/1915	17/09/1915
War Diary	Albert	18/09/1915	30/09/1915
Heading	18th Division 79th F.C.R.E. Vol 4 Oct 15		
War Diary	Albert	01/10/1915	31/10/1915
Heading	18th Division 79th F.C.R.E. Vol 5 Dec 15		
War Diary	Albert	01/11/1915	30/11/1915
Heading	18th Division 79th F.C.R.E. Vol 6 Decr 15		
War Diary	Albert	01/12/1915	31/12/1915
Heading	79th F.C.R.E. Vol 7		
War Diary	Albert	01/01/1916	29/02/1916
Heading	79th Field By R.E Vol VIII		
Miscellaneous	To O/C R.E Base Records D.A.G. G.H.O 3rd Echelon	03/03/1916	03/03/1916
Heading	79 F.C.R.E Vol 9		
War Diary	Albert	01/03/1916	04/03/1916
War Diary	Laneuville	05/03/1916	10/03/1916
War Diary	Bray	11/03/1916	25/06/1916
War Diary	Billon Wood	24/06/1916	30/06/1916
Miscellaneous	C.R.S 18	02/08/1916	02/08/1916
Miscellaneous			
Miscellaneous		01/06/1916	01/06/1916
Miscellaneous	A Form. Messages And Signals.		
War Diary	Billon Wood	01/07/1916	03/07/1916
Miscellaneous	DAAG (1) Forwarded as this is apparently an Original Copy	20/07/1916	20/07/1916
War Diary	Carnoy	04/07/1916	07/07/1916
War Diary	Bray	08/07/1916	10/07/1916
War Diary	Bray Camp	11/07/1916	13/07/1916
War Diary	Corse Valley	14/07/1916	19/07/1916
War Diary	Bray Camp	20/07/1916	21/07/1916
War Diary	Hocquin Court	22/07/1916	23/07/1916
War Diary	Staple	24/07/1916	28/07/1916
War Diary	St Jans Cappel	29/07/1916	31/07/1916
Heading	79th Field Company, R.E Vol 13		
War Diary	St Jans Cappell	01/08/1916	02/08/1916

War Diary	Erquinghem	03/08/1916	20/08/1916
War Diary	Croix De Bac	21/08/1916	25/08/1916
War Diary	Bethencourt	26/08/1916	08/09/1916
War Diary	Bouret Sur Canche	09/09/1916	09/09/1916
War Diary	Milly & Lealvillers	10/09/1916	21/09/1916
War Diary	Martinsart Wood	22/09/1916	25/09/1916
War Diary	Blighty Valley	26/09/1916	08/10/1916
War Diary	Outrebois	09/10/1916	14/10/1916
War Diary	Albert	15/10/1916	30/10/1916
War Diary	Tara Hill	31/10/1916	16/11/1916
War Diary	La Boisselle	17/11/1916	29/11/1916
War Diary	Ovillers	30/11/1916	21/12/1916
War Diary	Hautvillers	22/12/1916	10/01/1917
War Diary	Prouville	11/01/1917	11/01/1917
War Diary	Longuevillette	12/01/1917	13/01/1917
War Diary	Puchevillers	14/01/1917	14/01/1917
War Diary	Aveluy	15/01/1917	28/02/1917
Miscellaneous	G.R.S Div	03/04/1917	03/04/1917
War Diary	Aveluy	01/03/1917	08/03/1917
War Diary	Grandcourt	09/03/1917	11/03/1917
War Diary	Authville	12/03/1917	21/03/1917
War Diary	Vadencourt	22/03/1917	22/03/1917
War Diary	Rainneville	23/03/1917	24/03/1917
War Diary	Creuse	25/03/1917	26/03/1917
War Diary	Lambres	27/03/1917	19/04/1917
War Diary	Bethune	20/04/1917	21/04/1917
War Diary	Bully Grenay	22/04/1917	26/04/1917
War Diary	Vaudricourt	27/04/1917	27/04/1917
War Diary	Eps	28/04/1917	29/04/1917
War Diary	Beaurains	30/04/1917	30/04/1917
Miscellaneous	C.R.E 18 Div	03/06/1917	03/06/1917
War Diary	Beau Rains	01/05/1917	01/05/1917
War Diary	Heninel	02/05/1917	17/06/1917
War Diary	Souastre	18/06/1917	21/06/1917
War Diary	Ypres	22/06/1917	05/07/1917
War Diary	Ypres Zillebeke	06/07/1917	23/07/1917
War Diary	Dickebush	24/07/1917	18/08/1917
War Diary	Steenvoorde	19/08/1917	19/08/1917
War Diary	La Cloche	20/08/1917	28/09/1917
War Diary	Ypres	29/09/1917	31/10/1917
War Diary	Pilgrims Camp	01/11/1917	03/11/1917
War Diary	Boesinghe Camp	04/11/1917	12/11/1917
War Diary	Boesinghe	12/11/1917	03/12/1917
War Diary	Steenbeck	03/12/1917	03/12/1917
War Diary	XIX Corps Area	03/12/1917	03/12/1917
War Diary	Canne Farm	04/12/1917	04/12/1917
War Diary	Corps Line	04/12/1917	04/12/1917
War Diary	Boesinghe Camp	05/12/1917	05/12/1917
War Diary	Corps Line	05/12/1917	05/12/1917
War Diary	Cannes Farm	05/12/1917	05/12/1917
War Diary	Boesinghe Camp	06/12/1917	06/12/1917
War Diary	Corps Line	06/12/1917	06/12/1917
War Diary	Boesinghe Camp	07/12/1917	07/12/1917
War Diary	Corps Line	07/12/1917	07/12/1917
War Diary	Cannes Farm	07/12/1917	07/12/1917
War Diary	Camp B.b.c.2.8.	08/12/1917	08/12/1917

War Diary	A.11.a.6.7	08/12/1917	08/12/1917
War Diary	Cannes Farm	08/12/1917	08/12/1917
War Diary	Cannes Farm & Bruombeck	09/12/1917	09/12/1917
War Diary	Cannes Farm & Bruombeck	10/12/1917	10/12/1917
War Diary	Baboon Camp	10/12/1917	10/12/1917
War Diary	Boesinghe	10/12/1917	10/12/1917
War Diary	A.11.a.6.7	10/12/1917	10/12/1917
War Diary	Corps Line	10/12/1917	10/12/1917
War Diary	Cannes Farm & Bruombeck	11/12/1917	11/12/1917
War Diary	Baboon Camp	11/12/1917	11/12/1917
War Diary	Boesinghe Chateau	11/12/1917	11/12/1917
War Diary	Corps Line	11/12/1917	11/12/1917
War Diary	Cannes Farm & Broembeek	12/12/1917	12/12/1917
War Diary	Baboon Camp	12/12/1917	12/12/1917
War Diary	Boesinghe Chateau	12/12/1917	12/12/1917
War Diary	Corps Line	12/12/1917	12/12/1917
War Diary	Cannes Farm & Broembeek	13/12/1917	13/12/1917
War Diary	Corps Line	13/12/1917	13/12/1917
War Diary	A.11.a.6.7	13/12/1917	13/12/1917
War Diary	Cannes Farm & Broembeek	14/12/1917	14/12/1917
War Diary	A.11.a.6.7	14/12/1917	14/12/1917
War Diary	Boesinghe Camp	14/12/1917	14/12/1917
War Diary	Cannes Farm & Broembeek	15/12/1917	15/12/1917
War Diary	A.11.a.6.7.	15/12/1917	15/12/1917
War Diary	Cannes Farm & Broembeek	16/12/1917	16/12/1917
War Diary	A.11.a6.7.	16/12/1917	16/12/1917
War Diary	Boesinghe Camp	16/12/1917	17/12/1917
War Diary	Elverdinghe	18/12/1917	31/12/1917
War Diary	Boesinghe Camp	01/01/1918	01/01/1918
War Diary	Cannes Farm	02/01/1918	02/01/1918
War Diary	Elverdinghe	02/01/1918	02/01/1918
War Diary	Boesinghe	02/01/1918	02/01/1918
War Diary	Cannes Farm	03/01/1918	03/01/1918
War Diary	Corps Line	03/01/1918	03/01/1918
War Diary	Kuekuit Dump	03/01/1918	03/01/1918
War Diary	Cannes Farm	04/01/1918	11/01/1918
War Diary	Ney & Greyteayee Farm	12/01/1918	12/01/1918
War Diary	Steenbeck Broembeek	13/01/1918	13/01/1918
War Diary	Ney & Gruytuayele Farm	14/01/1918	19/01/1918
War Diary	Boesinghe	20/01/1918	24/01/1918
War Diary	Rousbrugge Haringhe	25/01/1918	06/02/1918
War Diary	Baboeuf	07/02/1918	09/02/1918
War Diary	Benay	10/02/1918	10/02/1918
War Diary	Remigny	26/02/1918	28/02/1918
Heading	18th Div. 79th Field Company, R.E. March 1918		
War Diary	Remigny	01/03/1918	20/03/1918
War Diary	Ly Fontaine	21/03/1918	21/03/1918
War Diary	Rouez-Wood	22/03/1918	22/03/1918
War Diary	Caillouel	23/03/1918	24/03/1918
War Diary	Varesnes	25/03/1918	25/03/1918
War Diary	Caesnes	26/03/1918	26/03/1918
War Diary	Autreches	27/03/1918	31/03/1918
Heading	18th Div. 79th Field Company R.E. April 1918		
War Diary	Gentelles	01/04/1918	13/04/1918
War Diary	Amiens	13/04/1918	13/04/1918
War Diary	Warlus.	26/04/1918	30/04/1918

Type	Description	Start	End
War Diary	Warlus Dieppe Map	01/05/1918	04/05/1918
War Diary	Agnicourt Amiens Map	05/05/1918	08/05/1918
War Diary	Diqc	09/05/1918	24/05/1918
War Diary	Bois Robert	24/05/1918	31/05/1918
War Diary	Henencourt Wood	01/06/1918	12/07/1918
War Diary	La Chaussee Tirancourt	12/07/1918	31/07/1918
Heading	18th Division, Engineers 79th Field. Company R.E. August 1918		
War Diary	Franvillers	01/08/1918	10/08/1918
War Diary	Henen Court	11/08/1918	21/08/1918
War Diary	Dernancourt	22/08/1918	23/08/1918
War Diary	Albert	24/08/1918	26/08/1918
War Diary	Mametz	27/08/1918	29/08/1918
War Diary	Trones Wood	30/08/1918	31/08/1918
Miscellaneous	Appendix To War Diary For August.	08/08/1918	08/08/1918
War Diary	Trones Wood	01/09/1918	01/09/1918
War Diary	Combles	02/09/1918	04/09/1918
War Diary	Fayier Wood	05/09/1918	15/09/1918
War Diary		10/09/1918	15/09/1918
War Diary	Nurlu	16/09/1918	16/09/1918
War Diary	Saulcourt	17/09/1918	18/09/1918
War Diary	St Emilie	19/09/1918	24/09/1918
War Diary	Maurepas	25/09/1918	27/09/1918
War Diary	Saulcourt	28/09/1918	30/09/1918
Miscellaneous	79th Field Co. Royal Engineers		
War Diary	Saulcourt	01/10/1918	01/10/1918
War Diary	Beaucourt	02/10/1918	16/10/1918
War Diary	Amiens	17/10/1918	17/10/1918
War Diary	Villers Faucon	17/10/1918	17/10/1918
War Diary	Premont	18/10/1918	20/10/1918
War Diary	Maurois	21/10/1918	22/10/1918
War Diary	Le Cateau	23/10/1918	03/11/1918
War Diary	Croix.	04/11/1918	04/11/1918
War Diary	Heck	05/11/1918	07/11/1918
War Diary	Maroilles	08/11/1918	17/11/1918
War Diary	Maurois	18/11/1918	18/11/1918
War Diary	Serain	19/11/1918	22/01/1919
War Diary	Clary	23/01/1919	18/03/1919
War Diary	Caudry	19/03/1919	30/04/1919

WO95/20271

79TH DIVISION

79TH FIELD COY R.E.

JLY 1918 - MAR 1919

121/6508

18th Division

99th F.C.R.E.
Vol: I

From 25th to 31st July 1915

as)
DyW

Nov' 15

121/6607

18th Division

79th F.C.R.E.
Vol: II
From 1 - 31. 8. 15

79th (Fld) Coy RE.

To
O i/c A.G.'s Office
Base

Herewith War Diary for Aug. forwarded as per Field Service Regs Part II.

[signature]
Capt RE
79th (Fld) Coy. RE.

1 9/15

Army Form C. 2118

WAR DIARY
or
INTELLIGENCE SUMMARY
(Erase heading not required.)

79 Coy R.E.

Instructions regarding War Diaries and Intelligence Summaries are contained in F. S. Regs., Part II. and the Staff Manual respectively. Title Pages will be prepared in manuscript.

Place	Date	Hour	Summary of Events and Information	Remarks and references to Appendices
Guildford	25.7.15	11.40pm	Paraded & marched to Guildford Sta. for entrainment	Apx
SOUTHAMPTON	26.7.15	4 am	arrived & entrained. marched to the W. Quay, at 5.30 pm embarked in R.M.S. Viper.	Apx
HAVRE	27.-.-	6 am	arrived about 11 pm. m 65= & disembarked 6 am. & boarded ship & arrived at camp at 6.30 paraded at 12	Apx
LONGUEAU	28.7.15	2.30pm	midday & entrained. arrived at station & disentrained. Started at 4 pm & marched to SEPTENVILLE via AMIENS	Apx
SEPTENVILLE	29.7.15	10 pm	& RAINEVILLE — arrived & into billets. went into billets. went into dirty billet is a farmhouse	Apx
"	29.7.15		Huts — water supply gave a ell of trouble.	Apx
"	30.7.15		billets	Apx
"	31.7.15		"	Apx

Army Form C. 2118

Original

WAR DIARY
or
INTELLIGENCE SUMMARY   79 Coy R.E.
(Erase heading not required.)

Instructions regarding War Diaries and Intelligence Summaries are contained in F.S. Regs., Part II. and the Staff Manual respectively. Title Pages will be prepared in manuscript.

Place	Date	Hour	Summary of Events and Information	Remarks and references to Appendices
SEPTENVILLE	1·8·15		Halted. aeroplane flew in vicinity.	
"	2.	4 pm	" " inspected by G.O.C. III Army. Sgt. C. Munro. proved with recruits when formed up of inspection	
MILLENCOURT	3.	10 pm	Very wet morning, paraded at 3 pm. descended 14½ miles to MILLENCOURT. 2 men & horse left behind sick in	
			SEPTENVILLE; 2 men related to work but one officer reported half day at MILLENCOURT, went into billets on arrival	
AVELUY	4.	10 pm	at 4 pm received orders to march at once to AVELUY. So sent on Capt WILFIELD to arrange for billets	
			& Company paraded at 7.40 pm. On arrival at AVELUY was met by Int. Officer. None of companies	
			house could be allowed in this village but after some discussion it was decided to keep	
			all the wagons & 16 horses & AVELUY, sending back to divine & 6 horses & MILLENCOURT	
AVELUY	5·8·15		Halted. 1 NCO went sick also LIEUT. A. WILSON. R.E. In the afternoon ½ Coy & 1 Coy & R. Sussex Pioneers	
			employed on bridge head defences of AVELUY	
"	6·8·15		Halted. In morning 2 Coys & 8ᵗʰ Norfolks this afternoon 2 Coys & 8ᵗʰ Suffolks & the Coy employed on bridgehead &	
			village defences. 1 drawn went sick	
"	7·8·15		Halted. ditto as yesterday but with 2 coys 8ᵗʰ Suffolks in a.m. & 2 coys 8ᵗʰ Norfolks in p.m. 1 NCO went sick	
"	8·8·15		Halt. In morning Coy + 2 coys 8 Norfolks employed on bridge head & village defences. In afternoon Coy only worked	
"	9·8·15		" " " " + 2 " 8 Norfolks " " " "	
"	10·8·15		Halt. In morning Coy + 2 coys 8 Norfolks " " " " " — bridge head & village defences. In afternoon Coy only worked	
"	11·8·		" " + 2 " " " " " " " " " " " " " Coy + 2 coys 8	
"	12·8		Halt. in morning Coy + 2 coys Norfolks + 2 coys Sussex Pioneers employed on bridge head & village defences. In afternoon	
			" " " " " " " & R. Sussex Pioneers. R. Sussex Pioneers worked	
"	13·8·15		Halt. 2 men came back from hospital. Coy + 2 coys 8. R. Sussex Pioneers worked from 8 — 1.	
"	14·8·15		Halt. 2 men went to hospital. Coy + 2 coys R. Sussex Pion. worked 8·30 – 12·30 & 2 – 5 pm bridge head & village defences.	
"	15·8·		" Coys + 2 coys Sussex Pion. worked on Bridge head & village defences. 1 Officer (Lieut LYNAM) went sick	
"	16·8·		" Coy + 2 " " " " " " " " " " " 1 Officer & 1 man returned to hospital. 1 man	
"	17·8		" Coy + 2 Coy Sussex Pioneers worked on bridge head & AVELUY defences. 1 Officer returned from hospital. 1 man went sick.	

WAR DIARY or INTELLIGENCE SUMMARY

Army Form C. 2118 (2)

August

Instructions regarding War Diaries and Intelligence Summaries are contained in F.S. Regs., Part II. and the Staff Manual respectively. Title Pages will be prepared in manuscript.

(Erase heading not required.)

Place	Date	Hour	Summary of Events and Information	Remarks and references to Appendices
LANEUVILLE LES BRAY	18.8.15		Marched via TREUX. 1 Officer (Lieut WILSON) 94 men went sick.	Nil
"	19.8		Halt. Reconnaissance by all officers.	Nil
"	20.6		Half started work on comm'n trenches with 2 sections to annexe A. 1 Sec'n sleepers dug-outs in annexe A. 1 Sec'n in night digging. Moved into billets [?]	Nil
BRAY	21.8		Half. Coy occupied with new billets & arrangements of RE Park. 3 sections worked in trenches in daytime taken at night, night digging. 6 C'y recruited trenches with 60 C.I.S. Bde	Nil
"	22.8		Half. 1 Sec'n on MINDEN Post in day. 3 Sec'ns & 1 Coy Someth[?] Pioneer & 1 Coy Inf'y on night digging comm'n trench.	Nil
"	23.8		1 Sec'n made hurdles fatigue. 2 sec'n employed [?] in comm'n trench together with 1 Coy Inf'y. 3 men went sick.	Nil
"	24.8		1 Sec'n made hurdles fatigue. 1 Sec'n camp fatigue. 1 Sec'n on comm'n trenches & hurdles at MINDEN Post. 2 men returned from hospital.	Nil
"	25.8		Lieut WILSON died in hospital at CORBIE	Nil
"	26.8		1 Sec'n made hurdles fatigue. 1 Sec'n on day rest. 1 Sec'n on comm'n trenches. 1 Sec'n undertaking Bomico [?] & camp fatigues.	Nil
"	27.8		1 Sec'n on HQ dug outs. 2 Sec'n on comm'n trenches. 1 on fatigues & making hurdles.	Nil
"	28.8		2 Sec'ns " " " 1 Sec'n making hurdles at RE "ship stores" in RE Park	Nil
"	29.8		2 Sec'ns on dugouts at MINDEN Post. 1 Sec'n making hurdles. 1 Sec'n at ship stores. 6 men arrived as draft for England.	Nil
"	30.8		1 Sec'n on repairing front line trenches. 2 Sec'n on making hurdles. 1 Section is moving at night digging comm'n trench. RE Park or Brigade Workshop started.	Nil
"	31.8		2 Sec'ns repairing front line trenches, 2 Sec'n on making hurdles fatigue.	Nil

18th Kurram

79ᵗʰ F.C.R.E.
Vol 3

191/7795

Sept 15

44th Field Co. R.E.

WAR DIARY
or
INTELLIGENCE SUMMARY
(Erase heading not required.)

Army Form C. 2118

September

Instructions regarding War Diaries and Intelligence Summaries are contained in F. S. Regs., Part II and the Staff Manual respectively. Title Pages will be prepared in manuscript.

Place	Date	Hour	Summary of Events and Information	Remarks and references to Appendices
BRAY	1.9.15		Half. 1 Sect on repairing front line trenches Left Sector, 1 sect on cookhouses etc WELLINGTON Redoubt. 1 sect on revetments and R.E. Pk. 1 sect on repairing rifled billets	
"	2.9.15		Half. 1 sect. & 1 sec repairing billets	1 sect. helping inf^y make dugouts etc
"	3.9.15		Half. 2 sects employed in C.1 sector & 2 in C.2 sector. 2 men arrived from base to join Coy	
"	4.9.15	"	C.1 sector & 2 in C.2 sector	1 man went to hospital
"	5.9.15	"	C.1 sector & 2 in C.2 sector	making dugouts & revetting inf^y 1 man went to hospital
"	6.9.15	"	1 sect. in C.2 sector	2 sects in camp fatigues, 2 men went to hospital
"	7.9.15	"	2 Sect. 1 in C.2 sector	1 sec sent to citadel to work under OTT in D/dest
"	8.9.15	"	1 sec^t working under R.E. pk. the other 3 sects went night digging the trench in centre of WELLINGTON Av. 1 NCO returned from hospital	
"	9.9.15	"	1 sect.	to R.E.Pk. D1 Owing to night digging & 8th Coy employed in R.E. Park on brick repair in afternoon.
"	10.9.15	"	1 sect.	2 sects in C.1 sector & 1 in C.2 sector on cookhouses.
"	11.9.15	"	1 sect^s	1½ sects in C1 — & 1½ in C2 — 1 man killed in action
"	12.9.15	"	1 sect	D1 1½ sects in C1 — & 1½ in C2 — etc.
"	13.9.15	"	1 sect	D1 returned to Coy in evening 3 sects in camp fatigues. 1 man returning from hospital
"	14.9.15	"	2 sects on C.1 sector, 1 sect in C.2. 1 sect in camp	3 men went to hospital
"	15.9.15	"	1 sect on C.1. – 1 sec. in C.2. 1 sec^t went to ALBERT as advance party. 1 man returned from hospital	
"	16.9.15	"	2 sects on loading timber wagon in R.E. Park. 1 sec^t in Albert as advance party.	1 Officer wounded 1 man went to hospital
"	17.9.15	"	2 sects	2 men went to hospital. Another sect went to ALBERT - 1 man
ALBERT	18.9.15		2 sections & H.Q. of Coy marched to ALBERT at 10 p.m.	1 Officer joined the Coy. Discharged from hospital, 1 man joined Coy
"	19.9.15		The Lt rested. Then made themselves beds etc	
"	20.9.15		Half 1 sec^{ts} digging cookhouses. Coy fitted huts in front line trenches & workshop in Coy workshop	
"	21.9.15		Half all H. secs out night digging on communication trenches & shelters. 1 Officer wounded. 1 man went to hospital	
"	22.9.15		Half Off^{rs} & 2 in sector E.3 making shelters etc 1.30H night digging on commⁿ trenches, 2 men went to hospital, 1 man come out of hospital	
"	23.9.15		Half 2 section in sector E.3 making shelters for wounded. 1 section in E.2. 2 men arrived on draft.	

Army Form C.21

WAR DIARY
INTELLIGENCE SUMMARY
(Erase heading not required.)

Instructions regarding War Diaries and Intelligence Summaries are contained in F.S. Regs., Part II. and the Staff Manual respectively. Title Pages will be prepared in manuscript.

September

Place	Date	Hour	Summary of Events and Information	Remarks and references to Appendices
ALBERT	24.9.15		Half 2 sec^n in E2 making dugouts etc. 2 sec in E3 making shelter for wounded & improving trenches	
"	25.9 "		" 2 sec " in E2 " " " " " " " & dugouts for OR. 1 man came out of hospital	
"	26.9 "		" 1 sec " in E2 - - - - - 2 sec in E3. 1 man wounded by bullet at night work	
"	27.9 "		" 1 sec in E2 - - - - - - - 1 sec in E3. 2 section rested & did coy fatigues. 1 man went to hospital	
"	28.9 "		" 2 secs digging new comm^n trench at night. overhauling tools & kits with remainder	
"	29.9 "		" 2 - - - - - " " " " " 2 sec^ts overhauling tools & sharpening them etc. 1 man went to hospital	
"	30.9 "		" 1 sec^n making crossings in comm^n trenches 1 man returned from hospital	

121/7431

18th Hussain

79 F.7.C.R.E.
Vol 4
Oct 15

Original – Army Form C.2118

WAR DIARY
or
INTELLIGENCE SUMMARY October
(Erase heading not required.)

Instructions regarding War Diaries and Intelligence Summaries are contained in F.S. Regs., Part II. and the Staff Manual respectively. Title Pages will be prepared in manuscript.

Place	Date	Hour	Summary of Events and Information	Remarks and references to Appendices
ALBERT	1.10.15		4 Sec'n on strengthening support line trenches. 2 Sec'n on carrying up bombs. 2 men strengthening support line trenches	
"	2.10.15		2 Sec'n on communication trenches. 2 Sec'n on comm'n trenches. 1 man went to hospital. 1 Sec'n on support line trenches. 1 man came out of hospital	
"	3.10.15		2 Sec'n on strengthening support line trenches. 1 Sec'n on comm'n trenches. 1 Sec'n on making burning places. 1 man came out of hospital	
"	4.10		2 Sec'n "	
"	5.10		1 Sec'n strengthening support line trenches. 1 Sec'n "	
"	6. "		1 Sec'n "	
"	7.10		1 Sec'n on water supply trenches. 1 Sec'n on strengthening support line trenches	
"	8.10		1 Sec'n " 2 Sec'n strengthening support line trenches	
"	9.10		1 Sec'n on water supply trenches. 2 Sec'n "	
"	10.10		1 Sec'n laying pipe on water supply trenches. 1 Sec'n on the morning comm'n trenches	
"	11.10		1 Sec'n " 2 Sec'n on strengthening support line trenches. 1 Sec'n " 2 men went to hospital	
"	12.10		1 Sec'n on comm'n trenches. 2 Sec'n on strengthening support line trenches. 1 man returning from hospital	
"	13.10		1 Sec'n " 1 Sec'n on engine water pipes. 1 Sec'n making dug outs to hops on trench. 1 man returned to hospital. 1 man joined two hospitals	
"	14.10		1 Sec'n " morning. 1500 thin iron stamping & complete to emp trench	
"	15.10		2 Sec'n on Am'n line trenches C 2 d 15 6.3. 1 Sec'n on cook house. 1 on dugouts in full line trenches. 150 thin stamping	
"	16.10		all Coy on putting up wire by night in front line trenches. 4 men joined the Coy. 1 fully requisitioned	
"	17.10		2 Sec'n on night wiring	
"	18.10		2 Sec'n " 2 men went to hospital. Requisitioned 30 sgt K steel pickets, 1 pulling machine	
"	19.10		2 Sec'n on night wiring. 2 men returned for hospital. 20 m betting 46 wire rifle. requisitioned	
"	20.10		2 Sec'n on front line defences. 2 Sec'n on redoubt (VSNA). 1 man returned to hospital. 70 pr lead piping 4.1 staff cutting machine requisitioned	
"	21.10		2 Sec'n on front line defences. 4 Sec'n on VSNA redoubt. 1 m Kilchner. 1058 per shuts or 1668 of sheets main stamping requisitioned	

Original

Army Form C. 2

WAR DIARY
or
INTELLIGENCE SUMMARY

(Erase heading not required.)   **G.W.R. (2)**

Instructions regarding War Diaries and Intelligence Summaries are contained in F.S. Regs., Part II. and the Staff Manual respectively. Title Pages will be prepared in manuscript.

Place	Date	Hour	Summary of Events and Information	Remarks and references to Appendices
ALBERT	22.10		2 sec" in front line defences. 1 sec" in USNA Redoubt. 1 sec" in cookhouse duties & fatigues.	Jno2
"	23.10		1 sec" in cookhouse duties & fatigues. In USNA Redoubt.	Jno2
"	24.10		1 sec" — 2 sec" in front line trenches. 1 men returned to hospital	Jno2
"	25.10		1 sec" — 2 sec" — 1 sec" in Redoubt. 1 Worthington pump ?!	Jno2
"	26.10		1 sec" — 1 sec" — latrine requisitioned. about 60 per in rest. 1 sec" in Redoubt.	Jno2
"	27.10		1 sec" — 1 sec" in front line trenches. 1 sec" in Redoubt.	Jno2
"			1 sec" — 1833 Kilos Rest plat	
"	28.10		1 sec" — 2 sec" in front line trenches. 1 Public wharf 16" clearin. 54" billeting-munitions latrines. 1 sec" in redoubt.	Jno2
"	29.10		1 sec" — sec" went to hospital. three relieved of hospital & rear	Jno2
"	30.10		1 sec" — — — klompling 39.5 K cooperate reguisitioned. 1 sec" in redoubt. 2 sec" in front line trenches. 30 metres dead before	Jno2
"	31.10		1 sec" in cookhouse duties & fatigues. 1 sec" in USNA redoubt. 12' leather tubing, 2 kilos dead fupping requisitioned.	Jno2

18th Museum

79th F.C.R.E.
vol: 5

121/7624

Nov 15

WAR DIARY
or
INTELLIGENCE SUMMARY

Army Form C. 2118

November

(Erase heading not required.)

Place	Date	Hour	Summary of Events and Information	Remarks and references to Appendices
ALBERT	1.11.15		1 secⁿ on water supply trenches. 2 secⁿ in front line trenches repairing dugouts &c. Recut cutter trenches + 16 Obs rear incinerated for hospital	Nil
"	2.11.15		2 secⁿ " "	Nil
"	3.11.15		1 sec " " : E2 + E3. 1 secⁿ in USNA Redoubt. 1 man new trenches bombing	Nil
"	4.11.15		2 secⁿ repairing front line trenches adv^d trench fallen in. 1 secⁿ USNA Redoubt. 1 man new trenches. 1 st " " 15' rev^t firing 4'13+3 filled iron ammunitions	Nil
"	4.11.15		2 secⁿ repairing front line trenches in E2 + E3. 1 secⁿ in USNA Redoubt. 1 man in hospital	Nil
"	5.11.15		2 secⁿ in front line trenches E4 + E3. 1 secⁿ USNA Redoubt. 1 carpenter. 1 cleaning markers. 40 feet trench propping. 1 man unfit. 1 hospital	Nil
"	6.11.15		2 sec " " making dugouts adv. 1 secⁿ in USNA redoubt. 2 propping +8 hosp.	Nil
"	7.11.15		2 sec " " " " "	Nil
"	8.11.15		1 sec " " " " 1 secⁿ in USNA Redoubt. 1 man sick. 1 hospital	Nil
"	8.11.15		1 sec " " B+ flat +60' trench revision & 125 sq feet	Nil
"	9.11.15		1 secⁿ on USNA redoubt. 2 men went to hospital	Nil
"	9.11.15		2 secⁿ on dugouts + trench pushing in E1 + E3. 2 men came out of hospital. 1 men went to hospital	Nil
"	10.11.15		2 sec " " 1 secⁿ in USNA redoubt. 4 m. water supply trench men. 1 man int^d hospital + 1 out	Nil
"	11.11.15		2 sec " " 1 sec " " " " " 1 man out of hospital	Nil
"	12.11.15		2 secⁿ " " 2 small chives. 30 pondures revision. 3 to fall to go to hospital. 2 small chives. 30 pondures revision	Nil
"	13.11.15		2 sec " " 1 secⁿ in Redoubt + 16 water supply + filler. 4 men taken to hospital	Nil
"	14.11.15		2 sec " " " " 4m water supply	Nil
"	14.11.15		2 sec " " " " " "	Nil
"	15.11.15		2 sec " " 1 secⁿ Mown Redoubt. 12 m water supply trenches & 150 ft. Any iron bars 1", and 7.0 ft. anywhere in water reg^t	M.F.
"	16.11.15		1 secⁿ Mown Redoubt, 1 sec^d water supply trenches on 1 sec^d Mown Redoubt. new water storage interior roofing reg^d only. My It. win buss 22nd Queens. Regt. no. 42613 Sup C.M. Leary wounded, shrapnel - transferred to C.C.S.	M.F. D.R

Army Form C. 2118

WAR DIARY
or
INTELLIGENCE SUMMARY
(Erase heading not required.)

Instructions regarding War Diaries and Intelligence Summaries are contained in F. S. Regs., Part II. and the Staff Manual respectively. Title Pages will be prepared in manuscript.

Place	Date	Hour	Summary of Events and Information	Remarks and references to Appendices
Abbeek	17th	—	2 Stations shelters, foot boards etc to front line trenches — Matt	AA
"	18"	—	" " " " " 1 sec" Marn Redoubt, 1 sec" traverse empty	AA
"	19	—	" " Sine plates, instead 13" channels, cut over roof. Iron grommets " " " " " " " "	AA
			Reg" 45 hides stone- papers " pulling planks 40 hides sheet - iron 22 ft iron trews 1½" × 1¼" —	
"	20	—	2 sections shelters, footboards ac to front line trenches. Reg" 1m old iron sheets 36" × 36" × ⅛" 1 Sec" Moira Redoubt. 1 sec" water supply &c.	AA
"	21	—	" " " " " " " } — 1 suppn in hospital. Reg" — 3 motors steam pipe, old	AA
"	22	"	" " " " " " "	AA
"	23	"	" " " " " " " } — Reg" — 30 ft of steel cable — ⅞" diam	AA
"	24	—	2 sec" shelters, flooring &c to front line trenches. 1 sec" water supply. 1 sec"	2nd Not
"	25	—	2 sec" " " 1 sec"	2nd Not
"	26	—	2 sec" " " 2 sec" water supply.	2nd Not
"	27	—	2 sec" " " 1 sec" in USNA Redoubt. 1 in water supply. 970 kilo sandbags in m. trenches. 270 jute hides. 140 feet iron rods requisitioned	2nd Not
"	28	—	2 sec" " " 1 sec" in USNA Redoubt. 1 in m trench supply. 450 k steel flats 4½ × 1 tons requisitioned 1 sec" in water supply. 1 m sheet + 20 m bars requisitioned	2nd Not

Army Form C. 2118

WAR DIARY
or
INTELLIGENCE SUMMARY   November

(Erase heading not required.)

Instructions regarding War Diaries and Intelligence Summaries are contained in F.S. Regs., Part II. and the Staff Manual respectively. Title Pages will be prepared in manuscript.

Place	Date	Hour	Summary of Events and Information	Remarks and references to Appendices
ALBERT	29.11.17		2 sec ⁿⁿ front line trenches, dugouts & boarding. 1 sec ᵘ on USNA redoubt. 1 sec ᵘ on wells supply. 1 sec bore down reqmnts	Apx
"	30.		2 sec " — — — — — 1 sec " — — — — — 1 sec "	Apx

18th Hussars

19th ZONE.
Vol: 6

13/7809

Decr 15

Army Form C. 2118

WAR DIARY
or
INTELLIGENCE SUMMARY

19th (Field) Coy RE   December

Place	Date	Hour	Summary of Events and Information	Remarks and references to Appendices
ALBERT	1.12.15		2 sec" on mining dugouts, claying platforms in front line trenches. 1 sec" on USNA redoubt. 1 sec" on water supply, workmen, roads.	Mt
"	2.12.15		" " " " initialing trenches. 80 tbs pd day requisitioned	Mt
"	3.		1 sec" USNA. 1 sec" on roads, water supply, trenches, tramways	Mt
"	4.		1 sec" " 1 sec" " 220 lb bombs requisitioned	Mt
"	5.		1 sec" on mining dugouts, claying platforms in front line trenches. 1 sec" on water supply, enclosures, roads, 2 sec" trenches	Mt
"	6.		1 sec" " " " " " " "	Mt
"	7.		1 sec" on mining dugouts E 3. 1 sec"	Mt
"	8.		1 sec" " water supply, roads. 1000 stakes 1200 pr hides requisitioned	Mt
"	9.		1 sec" " "	Mt
"	10.		1 sec" " "	Mt
"	11.		2 sec" test screen found 107 fr work in C.2. section. 1 sec" on water supply grounds.	Mt
"	12.		2 sec" working in C.2. section. 20 iron rod requisitioned	Mt
"	13.		2 sec" " " A 3rd sec" mounted over to follow 107 fr work in C.2. 14' iron bar 150 pd hides	Mt
"	14.		3 sec" working in C.2. putting up steel dug outs etc. Jalbert. 2 min repaired for Hitting.	Mt
"	15.		3 sec" " " & boarding trenches. 1 sec" " " water supply.	Mt
"	16.		3 sec" in C.1. making dugouts, tramways, trenches. 1 sec" Albert on roads, water supply.	Mt
"	17.		3 sec" in C.2. " 1 sec" " " Half Limbs	Mt
"	18.		3 sec" " 1 sec" " holes requisitioned	Mt

WAR DIARY
or
INTELLIGENCE SUMMARY

Army Form C. 2118

79 Coy/R.E. December

Place	Date	Hour	Summary of Events and Information	Remarks and references to Appendices
Albert	19.12.15		3 Secⁿ working at C.E. on dugouts & branching commⁿ trenches. 1 H^{td} on water supply, cookhouses, rondavels.	Nil
"	20		" " " " " " " " " roadside shelters	Nil
"	21		3 Secⁿ " " " " defences.	Nil
"	22		3 Secⁿ " " 1 Secⁿ on water supply, stables & cook house. 1 Section driving aqueduct bathroom.	Nil
"	23		3 Secⁿ " " 1 Secⁿ went to Bécordel. 1 man went to Buzies.	Nil
"	24		3 Secⁿ " " 1 Section bathroom, rondavel. 4 men with G.E. cookhouse. Albert defences.	Nil
"	25		holiday.	Nil
"	26		3 Secⁿ at C.E. on dugouts & branching commⁿ trenches. 1 Sec allied on water supply, cookhouses, rondavels Albert defences.	Nil
"	27		3 Secⁿ " " " " " "	Nil
"	28		3 Secⁿ " " " " " "	Nil
"	29		No a section	1 new	Nil
"	30		No 1 Section returned to Albert in evening. 2 sections in G. on dugouts. 1 section.	56 pieces corrugated iron & 6 6 boles zinc reqnd initialed. 1 secⁿ watersupply...CAPT CHASE. R.E. joined.	C.P. 6. C.O.D. C.O.E. 2.
"	31		2 sec^{ns} in Bécordel in E.Z.	

79^k 7.c.24.
fot: 7

Army Form C. 2118

WAR DIARY
or
INTELLIGENCE SUMMARY

(Erase heading not required.)

Instructions regarding War Diaries and Intelligence Summaries are contained in F.S. Regs., Part II. and the Staff Manual respectively. Title Pages will be prepared in manuscript.

Y9 ey Ful Coy. R.E. January

Place	Date	Hour	Summary of Events and Information	Remarks and references to Appendices
ALBERT	1.1.16.		1 Sec" on dugouts & E2. 1 on roads, water supply, billeting . 2 sec" & C.2 on dugouts	Put Put
"	2.1.		" " " " " " " " " " " " Gibberk. 2	Put
"	3.		" " " " " " " " " " " " "	1 Sec to mounted
"	4.		1 Sec " " " " " " " " " " "	Put from W107
"	5.		1 Sec " " " " " " " " on "	C.2. at theatre. 1 man iman hosp Put
"	6.		1 Sec " " " " " " " " " on "	1 on dugouts & E3. Put
"	7.		1 Sec " " " " " " " " " " "	1 C.2 " " E3. 1 Pulley shaft ANL dugouts C2 2 shoring E3 2 shoring (sec Purin)
"	8.		1 Sec " " " " " " " " " " "	1 Section relieved to ALBERT from C2 ANL
"	9.		1 Sec " " " " " " " " 1. on Usna & TARA REDOUBTS	IN E3 CaptSAFeb ANL 2 two battens transferred to IND.CAV.CORPS ANL
"	10.		1 Sec " " " " " " " " " "	in E3 dugouts — ANL
"	11.		1 " " " " " " " " " " "	— ANL
"	12.		1 " " " " " " " " " " "	1 man Khotels ANL
"	13.		1 " " " " " " " " 1. on Usna & TARA REDOUBTS	— ANL {forge bridging saws pullystock}
"	14.		1 " " " " " " " " " "	— ANL
"	15.		1 " " " " " " " " " "	— ANL
"	16.		1 " " " " " " " " " "	— 670 kilos ampers requisition ANL

Army Form C. 2118

WAR DIARY
or
INTELLIGENCE SUMMARY

(Erase heading not required.)

49th (?) Div RE   January

Instructions regarding War Diaries and Intelligence Summaries are contained in F.S. Regs., Part II. and the Staff Manual respectively. Title Pages will be prepared in manuscript.

Place	Date	Hour	Summary of Events and Information	Remarks and references to Appendices
ALBERT	17.1.16		1 sec^n building USNA & TARA R2 dug outs. 1 sec^n dug outs MG emp. E3. 1 sec^n dug outs MG emp E2. 1 sec^n ALBERT Defences.	Regulation Uniform Sheancock. ANZ
"	18.1.16		"	
"	19.1.16		"	Boots plate requisition } ANZ
"	20.1.16		"	1 man wounded to hospital. 1 man illness gone to hospital. } ANZ
"	21.1.16		sec^n resting USNA & TARA.	
"	22.1.16		"	
"	23.1.16		"	A/Cheer
"	24.1.16		"	{1 Battn plate requisition. 1 man in Border reconciliation. PPL
"	25.1.16		resting	eople
"	26.1.16		resting. 1 man to hospital	eople
"	27.1.16		resting	C.C.R. eople
"	28.1.16		resting	C.C.R. eople
"	29.1.16		dugouts sec E2	C.C.R. eople
"	30.1.16		resting	1 man to hospital. eople
"	31.1.16		dugouts sec E3	resting. Albert defence. eople

WAR DIARY

Army Form C. 2118

INTELLIGENCE SUMMARY

February 79th Field Coy R.E.

(Erase heading not required.)

Place	Date	Hour	Summary of Events and Information	Remarks and references to Appendices
Albert	1.2.16		1 sect. dugouts + M.G. emplacements E2; 1 sect. dug-outs + M.G. emplacements E3; 1 sect. roads water-supply	e.g.e.
"	2.2.16		3 sects. laying out and digging advanced trench E3; 1 sect. baths, roads, + dug-outs	e.g.e
"	3.2.16		3 sects	e.g.e
"	4.2.16		1 sect. dug-out + M.G. emplacements E3; 1 sect. dug-outs + M.G. emplacements E3; 1 sect. baths	e.g.e.
"	5.2.16		a " "	e.g.e.
"	6.2.16		resting	e.g.e.
"	7.2.16		1 sect. dug-outs + M.G. emplacements E3	e.g.e.
"	8.2.16		"	e.g.e.
"	9.2.16		"	e.g.e.
"	10.2.16		"	e.g.e.
"	11.2.16		"	e.g.e.
"	12.2.16		"	e.g.e.
"	13.2.16		"	e.g.e.
"	14.2.16		practising	e.g.e.
"	15.2.16		dug-outs + M.G. emplacements E3	e.g.e.
"	16.2.16		"	e.g.e.
"	17.2.16		"	e.g.e.
"	18.2.16		dug-outs E3	e.g.e.
"	19.2.16		"	e.g.e
"	20.2.16		"	e.g.e
"	21.2.16		"	e.g.e
"	22.2.16		"	e.g.e
"	23.2.16		resting	e.g.e
"	24.2.16		dugouts E3	e.g.e
"	25.2.16		"	e.g.e
"	26.2.16		"	e.g.e
"	27.2.16		"	e.g.e
"	28.2.16		"	e.g.e
"	29.2.16		"	e.g.e

79th Field Coy R.E.

Vol VIII

To O/c R.E. Base Records
    D.a.G.- G.H.Q 3rd Echelon.
    ─────────

Herewith,
      War Diary for the month of
February. Kindly acknowledge receipt.

1-3-16.   [signature] Capt. R.E.
              79th. Field Coy. R.E.

3/3/16

Vol 9
ج ٧٩ ع ٣

Army Form C. 2118

WAR DIARY
or
INTELLIGENCE SUMMARY
(Erase heading not required.)

Instructions regarding War Diaries and Intelligence Summaries are contained in F. S. Regs., Part II. and the Staff Manual respectively. Title Pages will be prepared in manuscript.

Place	Date	Hour	Summary of Events and Information	Remarks and references to Appendices
Albert	1.3.16		Section on dug-outs in about 3 meters Mami and three redoubts, 1 section wiring	
"	2.3.16		" " " " 3 sections leaving communication trenches. 1 wire returned from hospital.	
"	3.3.16		1 sec. went to Fauvilliers 2 sec. went to Fauvilliers	
Fauvilliers en Compte	4.3.16		2 sec. meeting	
"	5.3.16		meeting	
"	6.3.16		4 section drill with arms. One driver to advanced dressing stn. One officer att. 12th Divisional R.E. H. Q.	
"	7.3.16		One officer, 1 N.C.O., and driver, and have att. to 2nd 7th Div R.E. at Bray.	
"	8.3.16		One man rejoined from hospital, HQ 18th Division	
"	9.3.16		1 section, 1 subaltern, and Sergt. Sow to Bray 3 section wiring, rest in billets. R.E. One N.C.O. & 8 O.R. men 80th Div. attached	
"	10.3.16		3 section training, 2 or. man of 180 to A.S.C. M.T. roping, rest man of 80th Div R.E. rejoined their unit.	
Bray	11.3.16		2 " " HQ removed to Bray	
"	12.3.16		2 sections to Bray HQ. & 2 sections making camp.	
"	13.3.16		1 section working in Ranee D'Arbres	
"	14.3.16		" " " "	
"	15.3.16		" " " " 2 making camp	
"	16.3.16		" " " 3 " "	
"	17.3.16		" " " 2 " " 1 was to hospital. 300 meters reinforcement	
"	18.3.16		" " " 2 " " 3 reinforcements arrived.	
"	19.3.16		" " " 2 " "	
"	20.3.16		" " " 2 " "	
"	21.3.16		" " " 1/2 " " 1 reinforcement, 1 man out of hospital	
"	22.3.16		" " " 2 " " - one. shield, nephritis, leaving one	
"	23.3.16		" " " 2 " " " the first.	
"	24.3.16		" " " 1 1/2 " " Rest men very unfit and sent one man from hospital.	
"	25.3.16		" " " 2 " "	
"	26.3.16		" " " 2 " "	
"	27.3.16		" " " 1 1/2 " " 1 reinforcement, 1	
"	28.3.16		1 section wiring with R.F.A. 5	
"	29.3.16		1 section carrying from reserve.	
"	30.3.16		1 " meeting	
"	31.3.16		1 " Ladders & Workshops	

E.E. .... Capt. R.E.
79th. Field Coy. R.E.

WAR DIARY
or
INTELLIGENCE SUMMARY

(Erase heading not required.)

Army Form C. 2118

Instructions regarding War Diaries and Intelligence Summaries are contained in F. S. Regs., Part II. and the Staff Manual respectively. Title Pages will be prepared in manuscript.

79th (FIELD) COMPANY ROYAL ENGINEERS

XVIII

74 E/22 Vol 10

Place	Date	Hour	Summary of Events and Information	Remarks and references to Appendices
BRAY	1-4-16		2 Sections in manoeuvre on defence works/section on Gun Emplacements/return on general work, 1 man from hospital.	S/m
	2-4-16		do	S/m
	3-4-16		do	S/m
	4-4-16		do	S/m
	5-4-16		do/1 man to Hospital, 2 malaria/1 officer and 2 privates from R.E. incident.	S/m
	6-4-16		do	S/m
	7-4-16		do	S/m
	8-4-16		do — 1 officer joined from T.B. at Base Depot/ 1 man from Hospital	S/m
	9-4-16		do	S/m
	10-4-16		do	S/m
	11-4-16		do	S/m
	12-4-16		do	S/m
	13-4-16		do	S/m
	14-4-16		do /one man to Divisional School	S/m
	15-4-16		do / 120 ft timber requisitioned / one man in hospital	S/m
	16-4-16		do	S/m
	17-4-16		do	S/m
	18-4-16		do / one man in hospital	S/m
	19-4-16		do	S/m
	20-4-16		do	S/m
	21-4-16		do	S/m
	22-4-16		do	S/m
	23-4-16		do / one man to hospital, 2 6 mm (Auxillary) evacuated to base/ 1 man to hospital	S/m
	24-4-16		do	S/m
	25-4-16		do / one man returned from hospital	B.O.C.
	26-4-16		do / one R.E.O. from Div. School	B.O.C.
	27-4-16		do / see notes RANGEE D'ARBRES	B.O.C.
	28-4-16		do / do	B.O.C.
	29-4-16		Gas recon meeting auts + Nord ventilators, one —/—/ Ishigrove for O.C. H.Q	5.5.0
	30-4-16		Gas reclaim meeting	

1875 Wt. W593/826 1,000,000 4/15 J.B.C. & A. A.D.S.S./Forms/C. 2118.

XVIII 79 FCRE
MAY. VOL II

WAR DIARY
or
~~INTELLIGENCE SUMMARY~~
(Erase heading not required.)

Army Form C. 2118

Instructions regarding War Diaries and Intelligence Summaries are contained in F. S. Regs., Part II. and the Staff Manual respectively. Title Pages will be prepared in manuscript.

Place	Date	Hour	Summary of Events and Information	Remarks and references to Appendices
BRAY	1.5.16		1 section on dug-outs in Bray, 1 on RANGEE D'ARBRES position & tramway, 1 dugouts in BILLON WOOD, 1 camp work.	
	2.5.16			
	3.5.16			
	4.5.16			
	5.5.16		— 4 men on leave.	
	6.5.16			
	7.5.16		→ 1 training at Chipilly	
	8.5.16			
	9.5.16		2 men on leave.	
	10.5.16		3 men from leave	
	11.5.16			
	12.5.16			
	13.5.16			
	14.5.16			
	15.5.16		4 men on leave	
	16.5.16		2 men from leave	
	17.5.16		4 men from leave	
	18.5.16			
	19.5.16		1 officer on leave	
	20.5.16		{3 men evacuated, remained in back area on re sick list, 1 man resumed duties	
	21.5.16		1 man from leave	
	22.5.16			
	23.5.16			
	24.5.16		4 men on leave	
	25.5.16		3 men from leave	
	26.5.16			
	27.5.16			
	28.5.16			
	29.5.16		4 men on leave, 4 men from leave	
	30.5.16		1 man to hospital	
	31.5.16			

Capt. R.E.
79th Field Coy. R.E.

WAR DIARY
or
INTELLIGENCE SUMMARY

Army Form C. 2118

79. F. F. R. E. XVIII Vol 12

JUNE. 79. 1st 6. R.E.

Place	Date	Hour	Summary of Events and Information	Remarks and references to Appendices
BRAY	1.6.16		One section general work CARNOY, one sthg BILLON WOOD, one on Div. battle port one training in CHIPILLY	
"	2.6.16		"	
"	3.6.16		"	
"	4.6.16		"	
"	5.6.16		"	5 men from leave + 1 man on leave — 1 man to hospital	
"	6.6.16		"	
"	7.6.16		"	1 man on leave	
"	8.6.16		"	
"	9.6.16		"	Reinforcement arrived. 3 men wounded to hospital, 1 man on leave.	
"	10.6.16		"	
"	11.6.16		"	
"	12.6.16		"	
"	13.6.16		"	Section in reserve.	
"	14.6.16		"	1 man on leave	
"	15.6.16		"	3 men from leave. 1 Reinforcement	
"	16.6.16		"	1 man from leave	
"	17.6.16		"	3 men from leave. 1 Reinforcement	
"	18.6.16		"	Officer + 1 man from leave	
"	19.6.16		"	1 man to hospital	
"	20.6.16		"	1 man on hospital	
"	21.6.16		"	2 men from leave	
"	22.6.16		"		
"	23.6.16	2 sections Carnoy; two working in Bray		
"	24.6.16	"	" 1st Section moved to Billon Wood — 1 man went on leave	
"	25.6.16	"		

Major R.E.
O.C 1/9. 1st 6. R.E

WAR DIARY
or
INTELLIGENCE SUMMARY

Army Form C. 2118

79-4945 P.S.

June 24. 16.

(Erase heading not required.)

Place	Date	Hour	Summary of Events and Information	Remarks and references to Appendices
Billon Wood	24/6/16		The Company is attached to 53rd Infantry Brigade Hqrs. moved into Billon wood today. Artillery started wire-cutting. Nothing of note is recorded. The work for preparing the Brigade's attack is nearly complete. Light Stokes mortars have been dug in on the front line, mined-out chambers for gun crews & ammunition being made. All the ammunition is carried up. Light medium trench mortar emplacements have been made - and the 2" bombs carried + dug in. Two heavy trench mortar emplacements have been made. The ammunition has been carried, but only one gun has arrived so far. It is not in place yet. Two R.E. Dumps have been near the front line - and filled with stores. Three grenade stores have been made out near the front line - and filled with grenades. Storage for 800 gallons of water has been put in the front line - and filled. Three Batt. H.Q.s have been made two mined out and one deep tubular dug-out. Assembly trenches (4 including the front line) have been dug, and ladders and Bridges carried up. The work is not yet finished. Two S.A.A. and two ration stores have been made near the front line. Communication trenches have been deepened and boarded. In Carnoy the weather proof accommodation has been increased from 300 to 1400 men. Brigade Reserve ammunition stores have been made, S.A.A, wire, sand filled, Stokes ammunition and grenades. Brigade Head Qrs have been made in Billon Wood, for centre & right artillery & for the 53rd Infantry Brigade, these are deep mined-out quarters, mined-out dug-outs, with shelters outside. String Avenue dug and boarded from South side of Billon Wood to Carnoy. Carnoy to Billon Wood is nearing completion. Brigade observation Post has been made - also a long-range machine gun emplacements. No incident of importance to record the day.	

Army Form C. 2118

WAR DIARY
or
INTELLIGENCE SUMMARY

(Erase heading not required.)

19. Ud Co R.E.

Instructions regarding War Diaries and Intelligence Summaries are contained in F. S. Regs., Part II. and the Staff Manual respectively. Title Pages will be prepared in manuscript.

Place	Date	Hour	Summary of Events and Information	Remarks and references to Appendices
Bilton Wood	25.6.16		The work required to complete all our preparations consists in :— (1) Completion of assembly trenches, will ladders, bridges, steps out, sumps in, and some widening + deepening – These contain are working on this. (2) Some slight improvements to communication trenches generally – These are in hand (3) Squaring up of Brigade Reserve R.E. dump – (in hand) (4) Completion of LAPREE AVENUE. This should be completed tonight as sufficient boards are sufficient to get now. (5) A few minor jobs to do, and some more notice boards to put up – (We have put up several hundreds) No incident of importance affecting the company occurred this day	

[signature]

Major R.E.
O.C. 49 Fd. Co. R.E.

WAR DIARY
INTELLIGENCE SUMMARY

79th Field Coy R.E.

Army Form C. 2118

Place	Date	Hour	Summary of Events and Information	Remarks and references to Appendices
Billon Wood	26.6.16	6.30pm	One of the light trench mortar emplacements was destroyed this morning (53rd Brigade front). From evidence on the spot, I am fairly certain that its destruction was not due to enemy shelling, but to the explosion of a Stokes bomb inside the emplacement. Crew are buried, one of my sergeants and party are digging them out. Strong smell of gas. There is very little hope for the crew — the Stokes ammunition stored there cannot be blown up, and may be saved. I have gone up, and may be saved. No incident to this company worthy of note. My two "assembly" sections are resting in camp near Bray. My No. 3a is in B'llm Wood — my remaining two sections are in Carnoys working in the trenches. Assembly trenches are nearly finished. All the work of preparation is practically completed. There is some maintenance to do. The digging of LAPREE AVENUE is practically completed; but I cannot get gratings for it. Mane Murphy Major O.C 79th Coy R.E.	

Army Form C. 2118

WAR DIARY
INTELLIGENCE SUMMARY

(Erase heading not required.)

79ᵗʰ Field Coy. R.E.

Instructions regarding War Diaries and Intelligence Summaries are contained in F.S. Regs., Part II. and the Staff Manual respectively. Title Pages will be prepared in manuscript.

Place	Date	Hour	Summary of Events and Information	Remarks and references to Appendices
Billon Wood	24/6/16	7.40 p.m.	The Right trench mortar emplacement in which the explosion occurred yesterday was partially opened. Only bits of the contents could be found. The ammunition was found to be damaged. Two steps of these emplacements were reported to-day. In being hit by a 77 c/m shell. The stair unloaded a little owing to the heavy rain. From the same cause, the bridge over SPRING AVENUE had to shored up. The weather has been wet and stormy. The river has risen considerably. Trenches muddy & slippery. ---- My H.Q. is now complete in BILLON WOOD. My transport is in BRAY camp. No 3 Section moves from CARNOY to BRAY camp this morning, and has I & III Sections now. New BRAY camp to CARNOY. No. IV Section is in CARNOY.	

Adams Major R.E.
O.C. 79ᵗʰ Coy R.E.

WAR DIARY
or
INTELLIGENCE SUMMARY 79' 1st 6 R.E.

Army Form C. 2118

Place	Date	Hour	Summary of Events and Information	Remarks and references to Appendices
Billon Wood	28/6	6.0 p.m.	One Sapper wounded. (one man back from leave.) — No. 1 Section (Reserve Section) is now resting in BRAY camp. Nos. 2 & 3 (assaulting) sections are now in CARNOY. No.4 Section also in CARNOY. Very heavy rain has made trenches very greasy and very slippery and slipping. Notification of change of plan received. G. Bourdell trenches such as SPRING AVENUE, and EDWARD AVENUE are standing well. Unkeyed trenches such as LAPREE AVENUE are almost impassable. I have been unable to obtain yesterday's firm this trench. Two 100 gall. watertanks in front line parapets by enemy shrapnel. These have been replaced. [signature] Major R.E. O.C. 79th (3rd) Coy R.E.	

Army Form C. 2118

WAR DIARY
or
INTELLIGENCE SUMMARY 79. 4dc RE

(Erase heading not required.)

Instructions regarding War Diaries and Intelligence Summaries are contained in F.S. Regs., Part II. and the Staff Manual respectively. Title Pages will be prepared in manuscript.

Place	Date	Hour	Summary of Events and Information	Remarks and references to Appendices
BILLON WOOD	29/6/16	7.45 pm	Improved weather today; country is drying up. Front line trenches still very hot in places, and all untraversed trenches in very bad condition. — Entrenchment still continues. My sappers in CARNOY doing all jobs, widening a length of NIGNTADAN AVENUE, strengthening the roof of No.1 Report Centre &c. A Moore Major RE 25/6/16. O.C. 79th Coy RE.	

Army Form C. 2118

WAR DIARY
or
INTELLIGENCE SUMMARY

(Erase heading not required.)

79 Yd O R3

Instructions regarding War Diaries and Intelligence Summaries are contained in F. S. Regs., Part II. and the Staff Manual respectively. Title Pages will be prepared in manuscript.

Place	Date	Hour	Summary of Events and Information	Remarks and references to Appendices
Billon Wood	30/6	10.15 pm	No change in dispositions. No. I (Reserve) Platoon moves from BRAY Camp to CARNOY tomorrow morning — due to inire [entire?] trench 10.15 am. Weather now good — condition of trenches is much improved. [signature] Major [illeg] O.C. 79th Coy R.E.	

1875 Wt. W593/826 1,000,000 4/15 J.B.C. & A. A.D.S.S./Forms/C. 2118.

To
C R E 18 Div

Herewith
War Diary for the
month of July. Kindly acknowledge
receipt.

[signature] Major R.E.

79th (FIELD) COMPANY
Date 2/8/16
ROYAL ENGINEERS

O.C. 79TH

Headquarters,
18° Division

Forwarded.

[signature]
Lieut
2.8.16   for CRE 18° Division

HEAD QUARTERS
3 AUG. 1916
18TH DIVISION

materials
 Essex + P coys casualties about 7 each - but am not sure.

J Mamane

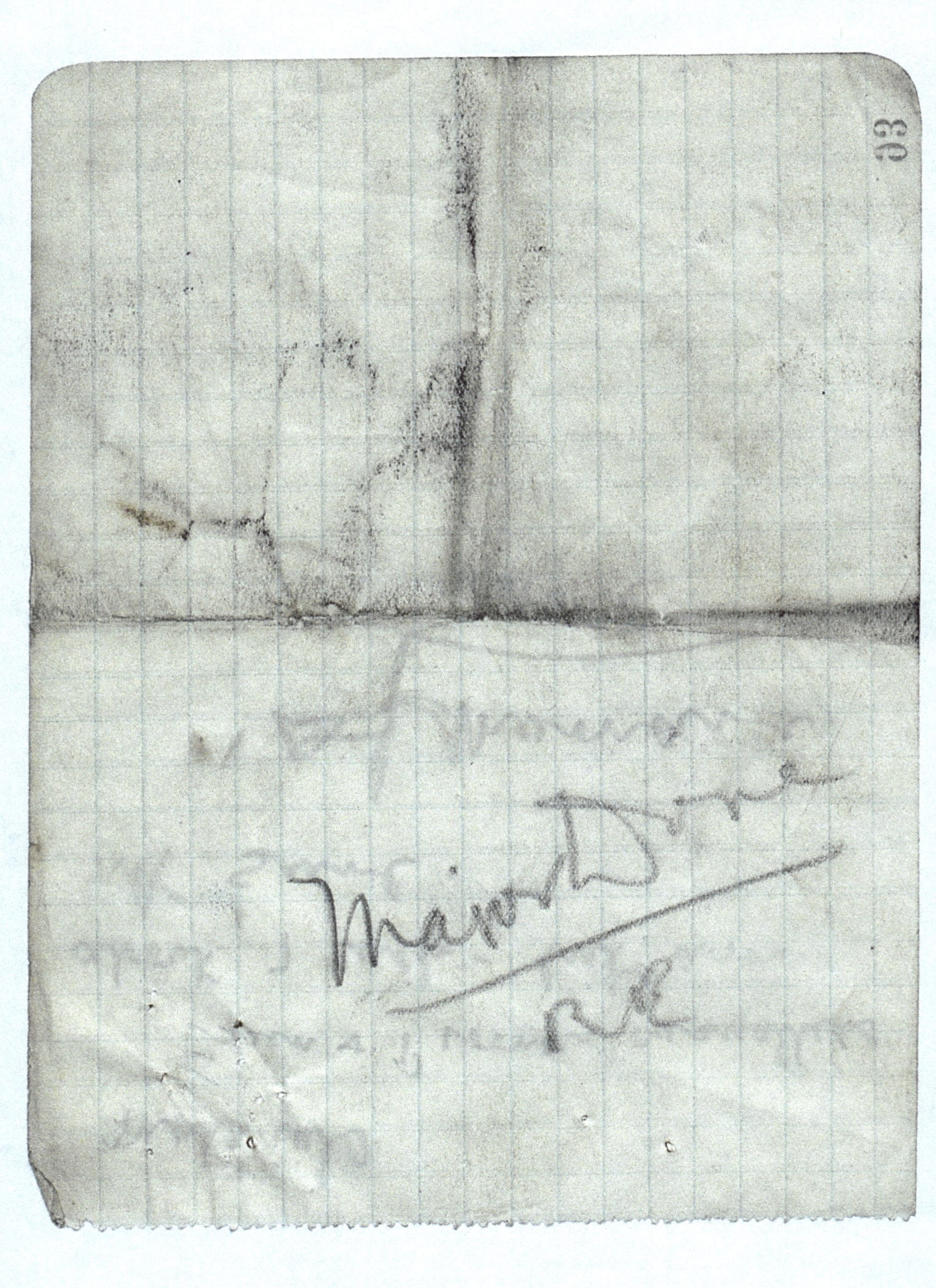

Major Done R.E. Recd 3·30 p.m.
                  6
                vr 1-16

Napier was hit here at the Look
                 badly - but not fatally
about 30 minutes ago. The
Infantry Officer I/C his carrying
party has also been hit — the
pioneer officer remains in charge of
party.

I and my pioneer officer
are all right. We were held up
here still about 12·15 p.m - as
a few Germans with bombs
and a machine gun held post
here. We have now started
with our strong point

Napier's people are here
converting Pommier Trench
into a fire trench. Has
Montauban & Montauban
Alley been taken — and
when will Napier's party leave
the forward to consolidate
it?

I have not had very
many casualties so far
— about 3 officers.
The Essex are proving a failure
as a carrying party — and
are not getting up enough

"A" Form.
MESSAGES AND SIGNALS.

Army Form C. 2121.

Sender's Number.	Day of Month		In reply to Number	A A A
* distribute				
~~damage~~ these	work	of	these
working parties	are	it	you
are able	to	do	so
Please inform	OC	Glasgow	I
have informed	him	that	you
would let	him	know	in
the event	of	your	going
up				

No J A Cochrane
CRE
CRE 18 Div

"A" Form. Army Form C. 2121.
MESSAGES AND SIGNALS.

TO { GRASS.

* C.   1/7   AAA

The Major General wishes the MONTAUBAN Rd put through for GS wagons as soon as possible aaa I have ~~instructed~~ Col Glasgow to send 3 platoons from the Boche front line to MONTAUBAN aaa you should send your reserve section to relieve WILSON's section aaa please complete with your men up to the German Front Line before going on aaa Please see your Brigadier and if he has no objection to your going up to do so should like you and

From ENGINE
Time 4/46 PM

WAR DIARY
INTELLIGENCE SUMMARY 79th Fd Co R.E.

Place	Date	Hour	Summary of Events and Information	Remarks and references to Appendices
Billon Wood	1-7-16	6.25 am	Bombardment started.	
		9.30 am	Information received that POMMIER TRENCH taken. Ordered 2nd Lt. Trumane to start for the LOOP with his entrenching party. Lt. Napier's entrenching party also started about now.	
		2.05 pm	Information that LOOP was captured turned out to be premature. Where parties had to wait for several hours. Lt. Wilson's section got to works on the MONTAUBAN road about 10.0 am. No.2 Section started then advance at the LOOP. Lt. Napier came up. No 3. section was employed at the LOOP. His section got to work on consolidating POMMIER trench, instead of their original objective.	
		4.50 pm	LOOP redoubt completed about 4.0 pm. 2nd Lt. Trumane commenced 2nd one at POMMIER LANE. This he completed about 4.30 pm, by which time the party were worked out. En III Section and party worked till about 4.0 pm; by which time they were even worked out.	
		9.0 pm	Lt. Wilson's section relieved by Lt. Holmes on MONTAUBAN road. He worked there till dawn; with Sussex Pioneers, had here entrenching	OB 49 Fd Co RE Major R.E. 79 Fd Co RE

WAR DIARY
INTELLIGENCE SUMMARY

Army Form C. 2118

49' Fed Co R.E.

Place	Date	Hour	Summary of Events and Information	Remarks and references to Appendices
Billon Wood	1.7.16		being shelled off the works.	
		10.0 p.m.	2nd Lt. Traverse took no Fy Section to entrench the front line. They were not able to do much before dawn - they came more heavily put down.	
		11.0 p.m.	I turned Capt Ingram at the L.O.O.P. - making arrangements for 2 Coys. of 4th Div. to entrench in in front. He had got 3 pontoon waggons loaded with wire up the MONTAUBAN road. I went down to CARNOY to meet them on return	

Sgd. [signature]
2/7/16

[signature]
O.C. 79th Fd Coy R.E.

WAR DIARY
or
INTELLIGENCE SUMMARY

Army Form C. 2118

79' Fld Co RE

Place	Date	Hour	Summary of Events and Information	Remarks and references to Appendices
Billon Wood	2-7-16	2.45 am	Two cmp. K.O.S.B's did not arrive at CARNOY until this hour. Equipped them with tools and materials. Directed me to the LOOP and led the others to MONTAUBAN ALLEY direction; but it became too light to use long routes, so dumped loads in MONTAUBAN road, near MONTAUBAN. Went to LOOP to find 2nd company, but could find no Frame of them. Capt. Ingram went to MONTAUBAN ALLEY, to help work of intrenching.	
		7.30 am	Lt. Wilson ordered to take nos. 2 & 3 sections to BUND SUPPORT, to make two strong points.	
		9.0 pm	Nos. 1 & 4 sections, with two Platoons Sussex Pioneers intrenching front line near CATERPILLAR WOOD.	
			Weather - fine	

Anne Magaille
O.C. 79/ B Co RE
3/7/16

Army Form C. 2118

WAR DIARY
or
INTELLIGENCE SUMMARY   79." Fd Co. R.E.
(Erase heading not required.)

Place	Date	Hour	Summary of Events and Information	Remarks and references to Appendices
Billon Wood	3-7-16	11.30 p.m.	Sections 2 & 3 marking about points in BUND SUPPORT line. Section 1 to marking about points they might work at MONTAUBAN ALLEY. 2 men in hospital.	

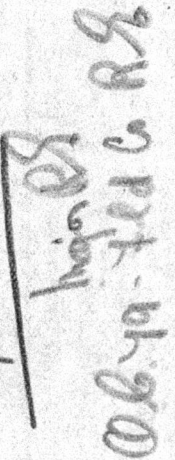
Major RE
O.C. 79 — Fd Co RE

Haig (1)

Forwarded: as this is
apparently an original copy

E A P Bowron
 b/Col R
10/7/16 h B E Vech

Army Form C. 2118

WAR DIARY
or
INTELLIGENCE SUMMARY
(Erase heading not required.)

Instructions regarding War Diaries and Intelligence Summaries are contained in F. S. Regs., Part II. and the Staff Manual respectively. Title Pages will be prepared in manuscript.

Place	Date	Hour	Summary of Events and Information	Remarks and references to Appendices
CARNOY	4/7/16	—	2 sections making road - wiring new trenches	
"	5/8/16	—	making strong points by night.	
			H.Q. 2nd — of company moved from BILLON WOOD to CARNOY.	
			2 sections digging EAST TRENCH to CATERPILLAR WOOD by night.	
			2nd Lt. R. Weir joined — and five O.R.	
"	6/7/16	—	All sections kept busy on entrenching and communications	
"	7/7/16	—	Company relieved by Cheshire Field Company - and retired to camp near BRAY.	
"	8/7/16	—	No I section in kitting - and putting for own trans- ports in workshops. Remainder resting and cleaning up. Much rain but kine things. —	
BRAY	9/7/16	—	Company resting and cleaning - Weather much improved	
"	10/7/16	—	No II section working on BRAY - CARNOY road. Remainder resting —	

Army Form C. 2118

WAR DIARY
or
INTELLIGENCE SUMMARY

(Erase heading not required.)

Instructions regarding War Diaries and Intelligence Summaries are contained in F. S. Regs., Part II. and the Staff Manual respectively. Title Pages will be prepared in manuscript.

Place	Date	Hour	Summary of Events and Information	Remarks and references to Appendices
BRAY CAMP	11.7.16	—	No. III Section working on the BRONFAY FARM road. Remainder resting.	—
"	12.7.16	—	No. III " " " " " " " "	—
"	13.7.16	—	Company in billets to rest it in front sector	—
CORSE VALLEY	14.7.16	—	Nos. 1, 2, 3, 4 Sections engaged to escape Valley & took over duties from 5 C Coy. During material former on BRIQUETERIE road at DUBLIN TRENCH. Nos. 3 & 4 Sections made dry weather track from BRIQUETERIE road to HAIRPIN and to TRONES WOOD. Three machine gun emplacements & machine gun dumps are GLASGOW TRENCH. On brought town a mobile Vet. Section.	—
"	15.7.16	—		
"	16.7.16	—	Nos. 1 & 2 Sections made dry weather track from MACHINE GUN WOOD to junction of DUBLIN TRENCH and BRIQUETERIE road.	
"	17.7.16	—	No. 3 Section ordered to consolidate WATERLOT FARM. O.C. was reconnoitred the ground and were engaging to making preparation. Until dark and were engaging light section in WATERLOT FARM when a German counter attack commenced and overran order of O.B. 16 at CHESHIRE REGT. Two O.R. missing and new men withdrawn by 5 3 & 54 St. Inf. Bde. This was too no one ordered to take part in attack on Guillemont to survived. Two men wounded.	
"	18.7.16	—	Sections moved back to GROVETOWN on relief by 35= Div.	
BRAY CAMP	20.7.16	—	Company resting in camp. All transport left at 4.0 pm for HOCQUINCOURT under Lieut. Symonds.	
"	21	—	Company proceed by march route to MEULTE and entrained. Named LONGPRE went 6.0 pm. Marched to HOCQUINCOURT	

Army Form C. 2118

WAR DIARY
or
INTELLIGENCE SUMMARY
(Erase heading not required.)

Place	Date	Hour	Summary of Events and Information	Remarks and references to Appendices
HOCQUIN- COURT	22/7/16	—	Transport arrived about 8.30 p.m. — Company partly in camp, partly in huts. —	
"	23/7/16	—	Orders to entrain at PONT REMY at 6.0 a.m. on 24/7/16. Company supposed to be at station at 3.0 a.m. - Parade at 6.0 p.m. to pack wagons and clean billets —	
STAPLE	24/7/16	—	Left HOCQUINCOURT at 1.30 a.m. - marched to PONT REMY and entrained. Left PONT REMY at 6.0 a.m. and arrived STOMER about 1.35 p.m. Left STOMER at 2.30 p.m. and arrived STAPLE about 6.45 p.m. Went into billets.	
"	25/7/16	—	Arranging billets. — and cleaning up. — &c. - One horse cast. —	
"	26/7/16	—	Mounted section, cleaning up and exercise. Dismounted, drill 9.30 am to 11.0 am. Company resting. —	
"	27/7/16	—	Same as yesterday	
"	28/7/16	—	Proceeded by marche route from STAPLE to S.T JANS CAPPEL	
S.T JANS CAPPEL	29/7/16	—	Cleaning billets - cleaning up. —	
"	30/7/16	—	Dismounted drill 7.30 am to 8.30 am Mounted - exercise & clean up. —	
"	31/7/16	—	Service	

18 Vol 13

79TH.
FIELD COMPANY, R.E.

Army Form C. 2118

WAR DIARY
INTELLIGENCE SUMMARY
(Erase heading not required.)

AUGUST (1)

49· Fld Co. R.E. No. 14

Place	Date	Hour	Summary of Events and Information	Remarks and references to Appendices
ST JANS CAPPELL	1/8/16	—	Inspection of R.E. field Companies of 18th Div. by G.O.C. Parade 10.15 a.m. in field near ST JANS CAPPELL. — One man admitted to hospital.	
"	2/8/16	—	Company resting. —	
ERQUINGHEM	3/8/16	—	Company proceeded to ERQUINGHEM by route march — 3 Sappers joined the Company (1st reinforcement). —	
"	4/8/16	—	No III Section detailed to take over ERQUINGHEM workshops and R.E. dump. — 5 Reinforcement horses arrived —	
"	5/8/16	—	No I & II Sections detailed for work with Div. Artillery —	
"	6/8/16	—	Ditto ditto —	
"	7/8/16	—	" " — The Sappers one pioneer reinforcements joined —	
"	8/8/16	—	No I & II Sections working with 18 Div. Artillery on all Battery Positions. No III workshops.	
"	9/8/16	—	No I & II Sections ditto, ditto and old jobs. — Ditto ditto. — Requisitioned for the length of 60 rom. shafting — 5 plummer blocks — one wooden pulley wheel driam 30 cents, width 7½" —	
"	10/8/16	—	Ditto ditto. —	

79th. Field Coy R.E.
Capt. R.E.

WAR DIARY / INTELLIGENCE SUMMARY

Army Form C. 2118

79th Field Coy. R.E.
.... Capt. R.E.
AUGUST 7/1/19 by R.E.

Place	Date	Hour	Summary of Events and Information	Remarks and references to Appendices
ERQUINGHEM	11/8/16	—	Nos I & II sections employed with 182 Inf. Anthem. No III section - 185 Div. R.E. Park. Kirkhope. No IV section. Wheels and old jobs.	
"	12/8/16	—	Ditto ditto - One sapper killed. One sapper joined.	
"	13/8/16	—	Ditto ditto - One driver admitted hospital.	
"	14/8/16	—	" " "	
"	15/8/16	—	" " "	
"	16/8/16	—	" " "	
"	17/8/16	—	" " "	
"	18/8/16	—	" " "	
"	19/8/16	—	" Sappers att. 80th F.d. Coy.	
"	20/8/16	—	Coy. relieved by 207th Fd. Coy. 79th Coy. billeted in Sorcie du B.A.C.	
CROIX DE BAC.	21/8/16	—	3 sections drills & camp duties. 1 section hutting for 34th Div. reinforcements joined.	
"	22/8/16	—	Ditto - 1 man to hospital.	
"	23/8/16	—	Ditto -	
"	24/8/16	—	Ditto -	
"	25/8/16	—	Coy. moved to training area & billeting in Bethencourt.	BETHENCOURT
BETHEN-COURT	26/8/16	—	Coy. training in billets.	
"	27/8/16	—	Coy. training in billets. Capt. & R. Harris R.E. joined. 1 driver joined. R.E. the R.E. the Depot joined at SDu anCRE	

Army Form C. 2118

WAR DIARY
or
INTELLIGENCE SUMMARY (3)

(Erase heading not required.)

AUGUST 79-Fld. R.E.

Place	Date	Hour	Summary of Events and Information	Remarks and references to Appendices
BETHENCOURT	28.8.16		Coy. on Bar. training with 53rd B. practicing consolidation in area B	Coy.
	29.8.16		Coy. on Bar. training with 53rd Bde.	Coy.
	30.8.16		Coy. training in billets	Coy.
	31.8.16		Coy. training in BOIS DES HEROMBUS.	

.... Capt. R.E.
79th. Field Coy. R.E.

WAR DIARY or INTELLIGENCE SUMMARY

Army Form C. 2118

79th Field Co R.E. (1) Vol II

SEPTEMBER

(Erase heading not required.)

Place	Date	Hour	Summary of Events and Information	Remarks and references to Appendices
BETHENCOURT	1-9-16	800	Training in musketry & consolidation	
—	2-9-16	—	— BOIS DE LA CARNOYE; 1 man to hospital	
—	3-9-16	800	Training in billets	
—	4-9-16	—	do	
—	5-9-16	—	do	
—	6-9-16	—	do	
—	7-9-16	—	Training with 53rd Bde, making strong pts & shelters in area B	
—	8-9-16	—	do	
BOURET-SUR-CANCHE	9-9-16	800	moved to BOURET-SUR-CANCHE	
MILLY	10-9-16	—	MILLY	
LEALVILLERS	11-9-16	—	LEALVILLERS. 2 reinforcements	
—	12-9-16	800	clearing billets & training	
—	13-9-16	—	Training	
—	14-9-16	—	in explosives, and plans – laying	
—	15-9-16	—	bridging, consolidation, found working parties	
—	16-9-16	—	Training; handing in Pontoons and 30 superstructure at VARENNES; drawing miscellaneous stores to replace. 1 officer joined.	
—	17-9-16	—	Improvements to Billets. Laying of Decauville track at 67 RE Park. 10 officers left.	
—	18-9-16	—	Lectures on foo and gas. Reduce in sections.	
—	19-9-16	—	making shelters for incinerators at LEALVILLERS; making tools. Bridge 9 cottes and shelters at 67 RE Park VARENNES. Making hospital at 2nd Field hos. 1 L.D.H. rejoined	
—	20-9-16	—	" " and shelters at 67 RE Park VARENNES	
—	21-9-16	—	"	
Martinsart Wood	22-9-16	—	Coy moved to MARTINSART WOOD; transport returned to LEALVILLERS. Forming dumps.	
—	23-9-16	—	"	
—	24-9-16	—	work in trenches	

Capt. R.E.
O.C. 79TH (FD) COMPANY. R.E.

WAR DIARY
or
INTELLIGENCE SUMMARY

(Erase heading not required.)

Army Form C. 2118

79th Field Company R.E.

September

Place	Date	Hour	Summary of Events and Information	Remarks and references to Appendices
MARTINSART WOOD	25.9.16	-	Preparation for attack. Assembly trenches begun by No 9 Div. Completed & others traced & dug by ration supplied by Infantry. Old German dugouts in HINDENBERG & other trenches were found out. Various other [illegible] (relic boards etc) were used. One horse wounded. 3 Reinforcements. Transport moved to HEDAUVILLE. One man slightly wounded. Still at duty. Carried out.	
BLIGHTY VALLEY	26.9.16	-	Coy moved in the morning to BLIGHTY VALLEY into BIVOUACS near Bde. Hqs. After the second intermediate objective had been reached No 2 Section (2 Lt B & 2 Lt Thurman) with a section of 1st Royal Fusiliers were finished up & constructed a Strong Point some distance out to the N.E. of THIEPVAL. The dugout was on first ground and when the Section arrived, probably from a Plumb Crump. Inside the former a sandbag wall was built up to save the other half. A serviceable German machine gun with ammunition was captured in the dugout & handed over to the garrison of the Strong Point for use there. A few prisoners were captured. No 4 Section (2 Lt Leslie Smith) were sent out to a point on Bulgar Trench to make a S.P. but on arrival there & this they could not complete the work as its position there was still being held by an infantry who had failed to reach their final objective. One horse to M.V.S. One man to No.1 (Shell Shock). One man killed.	
	27.9.16	-	On advanced dump of RE Stores was formed at THIEPVAL. By carrying parties from the Q. Roy d Berks & by the by Pack Pones in No 3 Section (2 Lt Wein) commenced on a S.P. on the W side of THIEPVAL, but could not make much progress owing to heavy shell fire. They also fixed wire & built 16 a mill in the village. The remaining sections improved & extended the track up the Nab Valley.	
	27/28.9.16	night	Tracing parties laid out in front & established the ZOLLERN-TRENCH for the assembly position for the assault on the 28— 3 Men to Hospital Sick & 2 men wounded	
	28.9.16	-	No 1 Section (2 Lt Holmes) + No 4 Sect (2 Lt Thurman) and with infantry Royal Fusiliers assembled at THIEPVAL or orders to make S.P.s at the CRUCIFIX N of THIEPVAL + in BULGAR TRENCH. Owing to extremely heavy hostile shell fire + the failure of the infantry to reach their objective neither of these points could be consolidated. No 3 & 4 Sections improved the track up the Nab Valley (2 Lt Wein) + No 4 Sect (2 Lt Wilson) + carried out some repairs to tramway in BLIGHTY-VALLEY. Whilst returned to bivouac. No 1 Sect extended PIP-ST towards THIEPVAL. No 2 Sect repaired tramway + secured bivilliers out. Casualties: 1 Officer killed. 15 other ranks killed. Two wounded (still at duty) 1 man sick to Hosp.	
	29.9.16	-		
	30.9.16	-	Coy placed by O.C.R.E. at the disposal of the 53. Bde. with orders to consolidate from points on the N face of the SCHWABEN. REDOUBT. 6 mms to the failure of the attack only one of these points was reached by the infantry. No 4 Section (2 Lt Leslie Smith) was sent out + constructed a double block in trench in Lucky Way. One man wounded. Two men wounded (still at duty).	

F. S. Thomas Capt R.E.
O.C. 79TH (FD) COMPANY. R.E.

WAR DIARY or INTELLIGENCE SUMMARY

Army Form C. 2118

OCTOBER

49 Field Co. R.E. Vol 16

(Erase heading not required.)

Place	Date	Hour	Summary of Events and Information	Remarks and references to Appendices
BLIGHTY VALLEY	1.10.16	—	Cleaning up Camp, refitching Bivouacs, making dug outs etc. 1 man rec'd from Hospital. 32 L.D.H rec'd.	
"	2.10.16	—	Work for 18th Div'l Artillery. One man from Hospital.	
"	3.10.16	—	" " " " " One man from Hospital.	
"	4.10.16	—	" " " " " One man to Hospital wounded. One man from Hospital.	
"	5.10.16	—	" " " " "	
"	6.10.16	—	" " " " "	
"	7.10.16	—	" " " " " One man to Hospital wounded.	
"	8.10.16	—	" " " " "	
OUTRE BOIS	9.10.16	—	Company moved to OUTRE BOIS.	
"	10.10.16	—	Inspections and training in Billets & reinforcements.	
"	11.10.16	—	Training in Billets.	
"	12.10.16	—	" " " Transport moved to HERISSART.	
"	13.10.16	—	" " " Transport moved to ALBERT. 1 man to Hospital wounded.	
"	14.10.16	—	" " " Advance party to ALBERT.	
ALBERT	15.10.16	—	Company moved to ALBERT. NCOs to trenches.	
"	16.10.16	—	Work in trenches. 1 man to Hospital wounded.	
"	17.10.16	—	Work in trenches.	
"	18.10.16	—	Work in trenches. 1 man to Hospital sick. 3 Reinforcements.	
"	19.10.16	—	Work in trenches.	
"	20.10.16	—	Work in trenches. 1 man to Hospital wounded.	
"	21.10.16	—	Work in Regina Trench. Work for Yanks". 1 man to Hospital wounded.	
"	22.10.16	—	Work on Regina Trench. 1 man from Hospital.	
"	23.10.16	—	Work for "Yanks", work on Pozieres dump.	
"	24.10.16	—	Work for "Yanks" work on Pozieres Dump.	
"	25.10.16	—	" " " " " " " " " 1 man at 18th Div Hqrs. 2 Reinforcements.	
"	26.10.16	—	Work on hutting for CRE - COURCELETTE Road - Pozieres Dumps etc.	
"	27.10.16	—	" " " " " " " " " " 7 Casualties to Hospital wounded. 2 LDH evacuated.	
"	28.10.16	—	Hutting for CRE - Work on Staff Redoubt.	
"	29.10.16	—	Hutting for CRE - making accommodation for 2 sections at Pozieres - starting hops for Courcelette Rd - locken Staff Redoubt, huyor works.	
TARA HILL	30.10.16	—	Cutting logs Courcelette Rd. Locken Staff Redoubt completed. Huyorworks. 1 hour from Hospital, 1 officer joining.	
"	31.10.16	—	Hutting Courcelette Rd. Company moved to TARA HILL. 2 Sections at POZIERES.	

R.S. Knight Major
O.C. 49TH (F) COMPANY. R.E.

79 Fd Coy R.E.
Army Form C. 2118

WAR DIARY or INTELLIGENCE SUMMARY

NOVEMBER Vol 17

(Erase heading not required.)

Instructions regarding War Diaries and Intelligence Summaries are contained in F.S. Regs., Part II. and the Staff Manual respectively. Title Pages will be prepared in manuscript.

Place	Date	Hour	Summary of Events and Information	Remarks and references to Appendices
TARA HILL	1-11-16	—	Work on Pozieres Courcellette Rd, work on trenching, making mud tracks, bridge for Artillery, minor works. 1 horse evacuated	
"	2-11-16	—	"	
"	3-11-16	—	Work on above and Gantries at Pozieres dump, work on Nissen huts. 1 man wounded to Hosp. 1 min to Rest camp	
"	4-11-16	—	" "Work on Baths. 107 hour ground"	
"	5-11-16	—	"	
"	6-11-16	—	Work on Nissen huts – Work at Battn ALBERT. Work at Dvl Sig dcot on dideint at Pozieres Dump	
"	7-11-16	—	" " 3 Hrs to Hospital	
"	8-11-16	—	" " 3 hrs to Hospital	
"	9-11-16	—	" " 2 men from Hospital	
"	10-11-16	—	" " 1 Section conflict with transport to ABBEY. 5 Reinforcements	
"	11-11-16	—	" " work at Dvl & Hqs.	
"	12-11-16	—	Work on Back Roads " " 1 Horse (LD) evacuated	
"	13-11-16	—	Work on Nissen huts. Work at Baths at Battn. 5 LDH incl.	
"	14-11-16	—	" " Work at Rd at ROCHE ALBERT.	
"	15-11-16	—	" " " " 1 horse to Base, Looked Bde Hqrs	
"	16-11-16	—	" " " " 1 Looked Bdr to Bde Hqr	
La Boisselle	17-11-16	—	Ready water and 1 section moved to La Boisselle. Work over Tramways	
"	18-11-16	—	Work on tramline " " 4 Reinforcements. 1 man from Hospital	
"	19-11-16	—	Work on Tramline. 2 men sick to hospital	
"	20-11-16	—	Work on Tramline	
"	21-11-16	—	Work on Tramline. 5 Reinforcements. 1 man to Hospital sick	
"	22-11-16	—	"	
"	23-11-16	—	"	
"	24-11-16	—	"	
"	25-11-16	—	"	
"	26-11-16	—	"	
"	27-11-16	—	Cleaning Billets and work on same	
"	28-11-16	—	"	
"	29-11-16	—	Work. No requests	
OVILLERS	30-11-16	—	Company moved to nr OVILLERS. Horse lines near L.A. BOISSELLE	

R Knight Captain R.E.

Army Form C. 2118.

WAR DIARY
or
INTELLIGENCE SUMMARY
(Erase heading not required.)

DECEMBER 1916

79th F.Coy R.E.

Vol 18

Place	Date	Hour	Summary of Events and Information	Remarks and references to Appendices
OVILLERS	1-12-16	—	Work on Corps Line. 1 Officer joining.	
"	2-12-16	—	" " " " "	
"	3-12-16	—	" " " " "	
"	4-12-16	—	" " " " "	
"	5-12-16	—	1 Riding Horse evacuated. 2 Reinforcements arrived.	
"	6-12-16	—	" " " " "	
"	7-12-16	—	5 Officers and men (Infantry) attached for work on Loop Line	
"	8-12-16	—	" " "	
"	9-12-16	—	1 Officer joining	
"	10-12-16	—	" "	
"	11-12-16	—	" "	
"	12-12-16	—	1 Officer transferred	
"	13-12-16	—	1 Officer transferred	
"	14-12-16	—	" "	
"	15-12-16	—	" "	
"	16-12-16	—	1 man killed – shell.	
"	17-12-16	—	1 Riding Horse received.	
"	18-12-16	—	" "	
"	19-12-16	—	Mounted Section moved by road to Puchevillers.	
"	20-12-16	—	Remainder of Company moved to Hautvillers. Mounted Sect. moved from Puchevillers to Beauval.	
"	21-12-16	—	Company arrived Hautvillers.	
Hautvillers	22-12-16	—	Work at Divl School 4 on tillettes	
"	23-12-16	—	" "	
"	24-12-16	—	" "	
"	25-12-16	—	Xmas day	
"	26-12-16	—	Work at Seilly, C.Sec. Hautvillers - la Jebe - la Motte Buleux - Forêt L'abbaye - St Nichola La Pote & Grand St Sulpice Carres	
"	27-12-16	—	"	
"	28-12-16	—	"	1 man hospital
"	29-12-16	—	"	1 L.D. evacuated
"	30-12-16	—	"	
"	31-12-16	—	"	1 mis to hospital

O.H.C. Smith, Major, R.E.
O.C. 79th. Field Coy. R.E.

Army Form C. 2118

WAR DIARY
or
INTELLIGENCE SUMMARY
(Erase heading not required.)

JANUARY
79th Field Co. R.E.

Vol 19

Place	Date	Hour	Summary of Events and Information	Remarks and references to Appendices
HAUTVILLERS	1-1-17	—	Work on LE TITRE AREA + R.A. area. Army R.A. detail at Chilly-le-Sec. 1 Man in hospital.	
	2-1-17	—	" " " " " " " " " " 2 L.D. Evacuated.	
	3-1-17	—	" " " " " " " " " " 1 Officer reinforcement.	
	4-1-17	—	" " " " " " " " " "	
	5-1-17	—	" " " " " " " " " "	
	6-1-17	—	" " " " " " " " " " 1 Section transport to Beauzincourt (No 3)	
	7-1-17	—	" " " " " " " " " " 2 men to Beauzincourt. 1 Man to hospital.	
	8-1-17	—	" " " " " " " " " " 1 Man to hospital	
	9-1-17	—	Sections returned to F. Co. 1 sick, 3 L.D. taken from Ransomes. Preparations for move.	
	10-1-17	—		
PROUVILLE	11-1-17	—	Company moved to Prouville.	
LONGUEVILLETTE	12-1-17	—	" " " to LONGUEVILLETTE.	
	13-1-17	—	" at rest at LONGUEVILLETTE. 2 Men to Hospital. 1 horse sick.	
PUCHEVILLERS	14-1-17	—	" Moved to PUCHEVILLERS. 3 Men to Hospital. Major Lewis found physically unfit.	
AVELUY.	15-1-17	—	" moved to OLD German Front Line - Nab Valley Rd. AVELUY.	
"	16-1-17	—	Repairing Billets (Shined dugouts)	
"	17-1-17	—	" " "	
"	18-1-17	—	" " " { Work on Communication Trench. Field + wagon. 1 horse destroyed. 5 Men to A.T.N. R.E. Dump.	
"	19-1-17	—	{ 2 Platoons Infantry attached for permanent working party.	
"	20-1-17	—	" Work on Communication Trench. 1 Man attached 182nd Tunnelling Coy. 2 Platoons attached for permanent working party.	
"	21-1-17	—	" Work on Communication Trench. 2 Men to hospital. 1 Officer attached.	
"	22-1-17	—	" Work on Communication Trench- Wagon- Field- Sudbury. 1 Man to Temporary Base. 1 Horse evacuated.	
"	23-1-17	—	" " " " 1 Man to Hospital. Major Builder took over Command of the Company	
"	24-1-17	—	" " " " 1 Man to Div. L. School. 1 Man reinforcement. (Vice Major Lewis) (acdours)	
"	25-1-17	—	2 Sections moved to MID QUET. FARM remainder on Field Trench	
"	26-1-17	—	Work on FIELD TRENCH and Opening up dugouts HESSIAN + REGINA Trench	
"	27-1-17	—	Cleaning up Linen Baths	
"	28-1-17	—	Work " FIELD Trench coleman " " " REGINA & opening up dug outs in HESSIAN + REGINA Trench. 2 men to hospital	
"	29-1-17	—	- do - - do - - do -	
"	30-1-17	—	- do - - do - - do -	
"	31-1-17	—	- do - - do - - do - Starting new dug outs in DESIRE TRENCH	

WAR DIARY
INTELLIGENCE SUMMARY

Army Form C. 2118

FEBRUARY 1920

79th Field Company R.E.

Place	Date February	Hour	Summary of Events and Information	Remarks and references to Appendices
AVELUY	1		2 Sections started work on dug outs in ZOLLERN ½ Section supervising work for R.A. & other ½ Section supervising infantry working parties on C.T.s HESSIAN to REGINA.	
	2		½ Section on NAB ROAD old GERMAN FRONT LINE. Transport near AVELUY. 2 Sections living in dug outs in MOUQUET FARM Company HQ	
	3		As on 1st. Small infantry parties due to reliefs. 2 horses arrived, 1 horse shot.	
	4		As on 2nd. Working parties delayed but still shot.	
	5		Work delayed due to enemy shelling. 1 P.O. killed, 1 Sapper & Pte wounded	
	6		As on 4th. (It been left our work of 67 Field Coy on Forward R.A. dug outs to dig into	
	7		No 3 +4 Sections with 2 permanent platoons in dug outs DESIRE, working in shifts, No 1 Section	
	8		+ on 6 in ZOLLERN, with 2 permanent platoons working in shifts assisted by daily platoons. No 2 Section on orig.	
	9		+ 4 on the R.A. working in shifts. Platoons work in 2 upper stokes	
	10			
	11			
	12		As above 4 3 Platoons W. Kents started forming before dumps GRANDCOURT.	
	13		From 11th.	
	14		As on 11th. Carrying parties for dumps DESIRE - GRANDCOURT.	
	15		R.E. on finishing off ch. in cuts & filling up R.B. R.B. 147 JHQ all permanent	
	16		Platoons carrying for dumps.	
			Settling in for battle positions tomorrow; 2 Sections & 2 platoons in STUFF REDOUBT. O/c Section + 1 Platoon in ZOLLERN trench. Some difficulty was experienced in finding room as orders were only received the evening before. Blew MOUQUET FARM as it belonged to a different armee brigade & informed that the brigade we were to work to give have always before to themselves & that the brigade are very loath to give up accommodation.	
	17		Zero hour 5.45 am. OC stayed at Brigade HQ but able it was very difficult to find out any definite news about the taking of the second objective. The tasks for the R.E. were detailed 3 strong points to cover the recent objective as the line had been taken meanwhile for the tasks	

Army Form C. 2118

WAR DIARY
INTELLIGENCE SUMMARY

(Erase heading not required.)

79th Field Coy RE

Place	Date	Hour	Summary of Events and Information	Remarks and references to Appendices
AVELUY	February 17 (cont)		3 Sections R.E. + attached Infantry + Applicants were made for the use of the garrison to help in carrying but this was not allowed by the division. Argument became very detailed of what stores were like carried up. All heavy stores were trundles were to be taken from forward dumps trunks the men but all small stores were to be kept with the section. Every man also carried up 10% shares were allowed as the group was very heavy due to the thaw. Both Officers + sergeants in each party were explained the scheme + had reconnoitred the route. Scheme was obtained. Good forward the section about 8.30am with orders to report to the forward report centre of each battalion in the advance defrent at the latest details of the situation as due to the counter attack the division on the right was held up. The front had left at 8.50am + the test about 9.30am, the difference in time being due to the time taken to reason the section. Messages were sent by 3 runners to make certain that the message got through safely. As soon as work started, messages were given that Infantry should be sent back with the time of starting, any change from the scheme, number of casualties suffered + if any special tools were required. Work on the first hut started at 11.25am, + the R.E. received the message about 1 cam. Messages were received in all cases by the second in command at Coy HQ + a copy was sent on to the Brigade, as there was intended to send the information. There was not allowed to leave till 1.30am behind the hut in the infront breaking hut in the front line till day the right + left try anything a little in between. Small enemy parties patrols protected the patrols at	

WAR DIARY
or
INTELLIGENCE SUMMARY

Army Form C. 2118

(Erase heading not required.)

Place	Date	Hour	Summary of Events and Information	Remarks and references to Appendices
APPELLY	January 17 cont		During the reconnaissance Rotating Guards on the right post attacked R.E. and approx. 4 I.N.G. were wounded. 1 R.E. Sergeant killed, 1 private killed & 2 wounded of the attached infantry. In parts of there were some of the digging had to be done by sapping due to enemy snipers. The third post evening the front into was in the selected location. Both officers + men worked very well especially N.4 But LANDON DR who got his job done although his attendant officer & R.E. Sergeant were casualties in the preliminary reconnaissance. The orders for the irregular part of the camouflage types started it. Posts later tried all round. Stores arrived not before the night post to hide the site. The last party returned 2 a.m. on the 18th. in getting up the Germans which were supplied by the escorting battalions. Waiting for situation before up in the evening laying duckboards. The giving was very heavy indeed due to the trans-duckboards, making the reserve working which had been kept back under the the case, they had been used in trenches.	
	18th		No.1 section returned to Brown Coy H.Q. and carrying shafts for M.G. teams in advance	
	19	a.m.	as on 19th	
		6 p.m.	No.4 section + platoon returned to Coy H.Q., leaving No.3 Sections + platoons in 2/11 RN	
	20th		train work on on 19	
	21st		All except No.3 Section + platoon latted.	
	22nd		No.3 Section + No.1 Section in M.G. shafts. No 3 Section in shafts for M.G. teams	
	23rd		Work on ROGERS Tramline on work in ROGERS Tramline	
	24th		await No.3 Section + platoon handed in to R.O.D. 1 Section to Maltese tent to Store. No.4 Section on gun pits twelve returned to 2/11 R.N. by No.1 Section + platoon	

Army Form C. 2118

WAR DIARY
or
INTELLIGENCE SUMMARY

(Erase heading not required.)

79th Field Coy RE

Place	Date	Hour	Summary of Events and Information	Remarks and references to Appendices
AVELUY	February 25th		1 Section + 2 Platoons on ROGERS Tramline, 1 section on improving Artillery entrances for RANGE. 2 sections + 2 platoons + 10 infantry on clearing road through GRAND COURT.	
	26th		3 Sections 2 platoons + two infantry on clearing road through GRAND COURT remainder as on 25th	
	27th		As above except 1 Section + 1 Platoon taken off road work on huts for the Division HQ. 500 .1 B Green. 1 no 8th morphia Aun proven opthalmic well indeed + a good night for Guns got through	
	28th		Arm 27th 11 Lt LUSSIGNEA 10th Essex attached to Coy on 27th to replace 11 Lt HAMIE wounded on 17th	

J.R.Sanders
Major RE
OC 79 Field Coy RE
05.3.19

Confidential

K565

C.R.E. 18 Div

Herewith War Diary for the month of March

J M Budden

3/4/17

.... Major, R.E.
O.C. 79th. Field Coy. R.E.

18/
Army Form C. 2118

WAR DIARY
or
INTELLIGENCE SUMMARY
(Erase heading not required.)

of 79 Field Coy R.E.

Vol 21

Place	Date March	Hour	Summary of Events and Information	Remarks and references to Appendices
AVELUY	1		No 1 Section & Essex platoon & No 4 Section & 720 Inf on GRANDCOURT–MIRAUMONT–E MIRAUMONT road. No 2 Section & Suffolk & Bedford platoons on tramline ROGERS LINE. No 3 Section & Norfolk platoon on filling up holes etc for divisional one officers joined Friday came with a field Coy. "Not G.S.M." left for course at Army School on February 26. 2nd Owens replaced 2nd WILLIAMSON with Norfolk Platoon on February 28th. 2nd LUSSIGNEA joined for duty with Essex platoon on February 27th.	
"	2	As on 1st	Transport lines moved from W/9 RANCES to E of RANCES near AUTHUILLE	
"	3	As on 2nd	Infantry on road only 520	
"	4	As on 3rd	Infantry only 450	
"	5	As on 4th	Infantry 300	
"	6	As on 5th	Infantry 450	
"	7	As on 6th	Infantry 200. 2 Sections + attached platoon lathing	
"	8	As on 7th	Infantry 300. 1 Section + attached platoon lathing	
GRANDCOURT	9		moving into battle positions. 1 section already in GRANDCOURT. 2 sections and 2 platoons went into dug outs in GRANDCOURT, 1 section and 2 platoons into cellars + dug outs in PETIT MIRAUMONT. CSM with 70 R. left in old dug outs with enemy kit etc. Zero hour 5.15am. The Company were allotted 4 strong points to make in front	
"	10		of IRLES & the GREVILLERS Trench. As the strong points were in front of the main line held by the infantry, it was not considered for the whole section + Platoon to all work by daylight, in the case of the most advanced strong point, only night work was intended. So it was proposed to take up the officers 2 NCOs & 10 O.R. from each section attached platoon (i.e. 5 RE + 5 Inf.) with picks & shovels + d tools by day & work by day & have parties to work by night for the remains	

WAR DIARY
INTELLIGENCE SUMMARY

(Erase heading not required.)

79th Field Coy RE

Army Form C. 2118.

Place	Date	Hour	Summary of Events and Information	Remarks and references to Appendices
GRANDCOURT	March 10th		who would bring up chiefly wire & pickets. Otherwise guides would go back taking men up at dusk. To get in front of our guns & a possible enemy's barrage in BOOM RAVINE. The advance parties was brought from GRANDCOURT & held in dugouts S of PETIT MIRAUMONT before zero hour. Orders to a personal reconnaissance by the O.C. two days previously, who had been able to get up quite close in a morning & get back in a second storm, the best means of approach & the possible shape of the strong points were worked out beforehand. IRLES was bombarded up to 6 zero plus 1½ hours 16.45 am. & it was known by doth runners & by some that IRLES was taken. Orders were sent at 7.0am from Battn to advance parties who arrived at Brigade HQ at 7.20 am. The parties for No 1 & 2 SPs went via PYS when they were detained for 1 hour before arriving at No the Sheikhs' lines & for No 4 SP via N9 IRLES, SP No 1 at G.33.a.23. No 2 at G.32.b.66, No 3 G.26.d.73 No 4 at G.26.c.75.35. Work started on SPs No 1 & 2 at 11 am & on SP No 4 at 9 am. The ground for each S.P. was 1/platoon I MG 1 LEWIS gun who advanced on the heels as soon as the objective was taken assisted by dug themselves in until the R.E. turned up when party of them acted as covering party. No 3 Post had no M G. 2 old German dug outs were found near the site of No 2 Post & as were brought into the S.P. The second one about 100x away should have been utilised	

WAR DIARY
INTELLIGENCE SUMMARY

Army Form C. 2118.

79th Field Coy R.E.

Place	Date	Hour	Summary of Events and Information	Remarks and references to Appendices
GRANDCOURT	March 10th	cont	but too much work had been done before arrival of R.E. to make it worth the charge. Various tasks were allotted to the S.P. o. in the case of No 1 & 2 by employing fire to from No 3 for all round defence & No 4 buried the sunken approach to IRLES. The main task was given to the M.G. & the work was sited for this purpose. Nos 1 & 2 posts were an irregular traverse to give to the front flanks & a short length to the rear. No 4 post was of the same form, but had the M.G. on a bank with an advanced post about 80 x 100 x in front on the same line chiefly for use by night. The main IRLES GREVILLERS road ran through this post. No 3 Post utilised an old Boche C.T. & formed a trench along the trench. There was a small detached post to cover the valley. The field of fire for No 1,2,& 4 posts was very good indeed, nowhere less than 200 x. The field of fire of No 3 was limited as it was sited in a hollow. Owing to a mist, work was partially with full parties on all posts 20 guncotton auxiliary for the remainder of No 1, 2 & 4 parties & the O.C. ordered up the parts for No 3 S.P. on his return. The O.C. guided up the parties for Nos 1 & 2 S.Ps. In my opinion it is very advisable for the O.C. or 2nd in command officer to get up as early as possible as in all cases various improvements were made before the work on the S.Ps had advanced too far. Few entire officers no always	

Army Form C. 2118.

WAR DIARY
or
INTELLIGENCE SUMMARY.
(Erase heading not required.)

79th Field Coy RE

Instructions regarding War Diaries and Intelligence Summaries are contained in F. S. Regs., Part II. and the Staff Manual respectively. Title pages will be prepared in manuscript.

Place	Date	Hour	Summary of Events and Information	Remarks and references to Appendices
	March			
GRANDCOURT	10th		Coy. have the necessary experience to clear the front out. The O.C. on the way back was able to make a reconnaissance of the GREVILLERS – IRLES – MIRAUMONT road over a hill on the barrage on IRLES. Work on S.P. No 3 started at 4.30pm. Finished 10.30pm. but due to heavy barrage they were unable to get back before 5 am. The parties for No 1 & 4 posts were very lucky in getting through a somewhat heavy barrage. S.Ps No 1 & 2 were completed but the other parties had to go up the next night to finish off wiring the road face. The section officer in charge for No 3 & 4 posts reported that the infantry did not want any more wiring done <del>installations</del>. Probably only a 2nd Lieut was in charge. 2nd work. The O.C. had seen the situation himself & sent up the parties the next night. <del>reconnaissance party & wiring party</del>. 4 I.D. horses received, the total amounts received up to now	
	11th		completed S.Ps No 3 & 4. 2 platoons clearing road in front of Brigade HQ. 2 sections improving dug-out so they would be required for the Battalion Coy HQ for the next operations.	
AUTHUILLE	12th		Took over from 80th Field Coy RE. No 4 Section & Berkshire platoon left in GRANDCOURT. Nos 1 & 2 Sections & Essex platoon AVELUY dump with a detachment Coy HQ No 3 Section & Norfolk & Suffolk platoons at AUTHUILLE where transport & horse lines of the RE had previously been sent on to. 12 men at O.T. Quad(?)	13A

T.P.134. W.t. W708-776. 500000. 4/15. Sir J. C. & S.

Army Form C. 2118.

WAR DIARY
or
INTELLIGENCE SUMMARY.
(Erase heading not required.)

79th Field Coy R.E.

Instructions regarding War Diaries and Intelligence Summaries are contained in F.S. Regs., Part II. and the Staff Manual respectively. Title pages will be prepared in manuscript.

Place	Date	Hour	Summary of Events and Information	Remarks and references to Appendices
	March			
AUTHUILLE	13th		Nos 1 & 2 Sections & Coys platoon on AVELUY & O.T. dumps. No 3 Section on agricult[ural] platoon in divisional H.Q. No 4 Section & Berkshire platoon on road through GRANDCOURT. Supply platoon & p.m. clearing up the camp. 1/2 wheat O.T.D. 100 Inf on GRANDCOURT road.	
"	14th		As on 13th except 1/2 Supplies loading sleepers on 10 G.S. wagons for GRANDCOURT road. Inclined fut at O.T.D. 4 North reinforcements arrived for platoon	
"	15		As on 14th. Italian Supplies work in camp. No Sections talked blanket shirts sterilized 200 Inf on road	
"	16		As on 15th. Nos 3 sections completed & platoons talked & blankets sterilized. 200 Inf on road. No 3 section completed stables for Div H.Q.	
"	17		As on 16th. No 3 Section platoon returned for dinner, afterwards good drill & inspection by O.C. 200 Inf on road.	
"	18		Nos 1,2 & 4 Section platoon as before. No 3 Section platoon moved to MIRAUMONT. Before moving loaded harlows for 85th Field Coy R.E. 100 Inf on road	
"	19		Nos 1,2 & 4 Sections as before. 100 Inf on road. No 3 Section on road through PYS with 200 Germans	
"	20		No 1 & 2 Sections howsing out church. Nos 3 & 4 Section with 2 Coys Pioneers on GRANDCOURT road. Lifts with sections reported by H.Q. Wire netting platoon & reserve Brigade sent 10 p.m. No 19th reserve 11.18am No 20th. Platoons reported Brigade at WARLOY late Col 2nd 8th Company preparing to move on 21st	

WAR DIARY / INTELLIGENCE SUMMARY

Army Form C. 2118.

79th Field Coy R.E.

Place	Date	Hour	Summary of Events and Information	Remarks and references to Appendices
	March			
AUTHUILLE	21st		Orders to leave S.P. at 7.0 am. Received at 8.0 am. Passed S.P. at 9.0 am. & cut into 55th Inf Bde with whom we had orders to march. Billets Chateau VADENCOURT (good)	
VADENCOURT	22nd		Marched with 53rd Inf Bde. Billets RAINNEVILLE. Draught horses in open	
RAINNEVILLE	23rd		Halt. Cleaning wagons etc. Company inspected by O.C.	
	24th		Dismounted under O.C. marched to VILLERS BOCAGE & thence by motor buses to CREUSE. Transport by road under 2nd Lieut LADDEN. Cyclists under Lieut WEIR WHOLLATT. Delay of 4 hrs at VILLERS BOCAGE. Billets at CHATEAU (good)	
CREUSE	25th		Orders at 1.30 am to be at BOCAEL at 4.0 am. for entraining. Arrived to time & had to halt till 9.0 am. doing nothing whilst 2 trains loaded up. Book staff work as it was quite impossible to make up 4 hrs in 2 trains when first train left 6 hrs or more late. Entrained in 1 hour with 1 Coy 8th Suffolks & A.S.C. Left 10.45 am. First Summer time started on night of 24/25th. Advance party at HAZNES 6 O.R. & 3 bicycles by 1st train. Arrived BERGEETTE at 5.30 p.m. marched off within 1 hour of arrival. Very slow journey. At one time 5 trains were found up waiting to get along.	
	26th			
LAMBRES	27th		Billets for men horses in Le HAMEL. Coy HQ in LAMBRES. Left 6th Dn R Berks at 6th F. Ambulance. Settling in, cleaning wagons, equipment etc. 3 mounted & 8 dismounted reinforcements joined on 25th morning	

Army Form C. 2118.

WAR DIARY
~~INTELLIGENCE~~ SUMMARY
79th Field Coy R.E.

(Erase heading not required.)

Place	Date	Hour	Summary of Events and Information	Remarks and references to Appendices
	March			
LAMBRES	28		Training in morning, rest afternoon, one reinforcement joined	
"	29		As on 28th. Kit rifle inspection.	
"	30		Route march. Rifle inspection on return.	
"	31		Company training. Box respirators tested in gas chamber. 3 reinforcements joined.	

J.M. Brothers
Major R.E.
O.C. 79 Field Coy R.E.

79 Fd Coy R.E.

WAR DIARY
INTELLIGENCE SUMMARY.
APRIL.

Place	Date	Hour	Summary of Events and Information	Remarks and references to Appendices
LAMBRES	April 1st		Inspection of saddlery by OC No 1 Section showed the last two out (condemned)	
"	2		Inspection of company by O.C. 18th Div. 4 CRE. while at training. Inspection of HQ mounted portion. Trestle teams altered less time not of movement.	
"	3		Overhauling of tools went month. 1 reinforcement arrived	
"	4		Company training. Capt. Knight rejoined company from course in England	
"	5		West library lodging school MRE. 3 reinforcements arrived	
"	6		Company training. 1 reinforcement arrived. 9/6 mules 8 horses were old, 2 sick. Corporals & Sappers awarded military medals for capture of TRUS's this sphere. Total of 1 military cross of military medals held by division held the trumps for the company	
	7		Company training	
	8		Baths. Inspection of billets Sunday	
	9		Company training (including practising)	
	10		Company training	
	11		Company training 4 reinforcement arrived	
	12		Company training	

Army Form C. 2118.

WAR DIARY
or
INTELLIGENCE SUMMARY.
(Erase heading not required.)

79th Field Coy RE

Instructions regarding War Diaries and Intelligence Summaries are contained in F. S. Regs, Part II. and the Staff Manual respectively. Title pages will be prepared in manuscript.

Place	Date	Hour	Summary of Events and Information	Remarks and references to Appendices
	April			
LAMBRES	13		Company training. Sub Lt Poole Naval Division attached temporarily for instruction in R.E. duties	
"	14		Inspection of section in full marching order + mts marcht. 8 reinforcements arrived	
"	15		Rifle + billet Inspection	
"	16		Inspection by C.E. II Corps + CRE. Satisfactory. Company training	
"	17		Company training stables	
"	18		Company training. Getting ready to move	
"	19		Marched with Brigade to BETHUNE. About 15 miles	
BETHUNE	20		Rest. Inspection of rifles + cleaning wagons	
"	21		Marched to BULLGRENAY. Attached temporarily to 1st Corps for work. About 8 miles	
BULLGRENAY	22		Went round proposed line of light railway. Section rigging out line. Sub Lt Poole left for II Corps.	
"	23		Work started. Men available 7 Field Coy, 560 A.T Coy, 180 Labour Coy, 22nd R.W Survey 240 Labour Coy	
"	24		Work on railway. In addition men available 4th B.W. 3. Regt 80 men, 11th Entrenching Bn	
"	25		Work on railway 2 shifts	
"	26th		Warning order received 12.30pm, but work to continue, 1st shift worked. Definite orders rec'd 3.15 hrs Company moved to VAUDRICOURT 5.50 pm. arrived 9.0 pm About 6½ miles	

WAR DIARY

Army Form C. 2118.

79th Field Ambulance

Place	Date	Hour	Summary of Events and Information	Remarks and references to Appendices
	April			
VAUDRICOURT	27		Marched with brigade to E.P.S. about 23 miles, men very weary but marched well	
E P S	28		Halt.	
	29		Dismounted portion marched to PERNES & went by train to ARRAS & marched to BEAURAINS where there were numerous old dug outs. Transport under Capt Knight & Lt Woollatt marched to HABARCQ. Both moves carried out with 53rd Inf Bde	
BEAURAINS	30		Transport joined ay at BEAURAINS. Men settled in	

J M Bartleman Capt R
a/ Major
79th Field
O.C. 79

To
C.R.E. 18 Div

K762

Herewith War Diary for month of May-17. Kindly acknowledge.

3-6-17.

F M Budden
................Major R.E.
O.C. 79th. Field Coy. R.E.

Army Form C. 2118.

WAR DIARY or INTELLIGENCE SUMMARY

(Erase heading not required.)

May 1917   79th Field Coy R.E.

Vol 23

Place	Date	Hour	Summary of Events and Information	Remarks and references to Appendices
	May			
BEAURAINS	1st		Dismounted portion of Coy moved to trenches SW of HENINEL	
HENINEL	2		Settled in. 1 Officer & 9 Inf Platoon joined Coy. Total 10 Officers 101 OR.	
"	3		Attack on CHERISY. Company in reserve but 3 sections attached platoon tents to S.W. Inf Bde. Before strong points on a right defended flank of runway. 3 Sections received orders to move up to a position of readiness at 6.20 am. In support trenches. On no reporting received orders to report to OC Battalion in front line. As a counter attack was expected, 4 men were not available in front line at the time. R.E. were brought up at 11.0 am to hold their support trench 100 yards behind front line. About 2.0 pm R.E. returned to last support trenches. A third attack at 7.15 pm R.E. were in readiness in case of necessity owing to the weakness of brigade in attack but were not required. At 7.45 pm have received orders that R.E. should be ready to consolidate new front line during night with 5 Sections of the other 2 field Coys. At 9.45 pm received news that attack was a failure & at 10.15 pm received orders to return to camp. Reached camp 11.0 pm. Casualties 6 of BERKSHIRE attached platoon buried but dug out unhurt. 1 Sergeant wounded in head.	

Army Form C. 2118.

WAR DIARY
INTELLIGENCE SUMMARY.
(Erase heading not required.)

79th Field Coy RE

Place	Date	Hour	Summary of Events and Information	Remarks and references to Appendices
HENNINEL	May 3rd		unfj — RE 2 O.R. knee & prince 1 Sergeant & 1 O.R. bruised & traumatised into shock. Remaining section with 2 Capt Knight received orders at 10.30pm to have a sunken road as near rivercut that Bosch were making a great counter attack. Returned at 12.30am as this attack did not come through. Due to information that our objection had been taken that division on right had failed we were sent up at 4pm along storny track the right extended flank. As it turned out that no attack had failed, R.E. were used as infantry. due both heavy losses of the 56th Bde. The men were under very heavy shell fire for 16 hours & had to bear through enemy's barrage twice. We were quite steady & helpful all the time when many others were very unsteady. Risk.	
	4th			
	5th		Work started on 2day onto for M.G. detachment & 2 double battalion HQ in front line, supervising infantry on C.T. & deepening existing safe of front line front — running forward to other safe 250ˣ - 300ˣ long on forward crest of hill & get extension of Boschi.	

Army Form C. 2118.

WAR DIARY
INTELLIGENCE SUMMARY.
(Erase heading not required)

7a" Field Coy RE

Place	Date	Hour	Summary of Events and Information	Remarks and references to Appendices
HENINEL	May 6th		Continuous shifts of dug outs & work by night on remainder.	
"	7th		As on 6th. One private wounded by 6" R. Bosh platoon.	
"	8th		As on 7th.	
"	9th		Left centre section taken over by another division so work on 2 left outposts of 1 dug out for a M.G. team and 1 double Bn HQ stopped. Work on a fresh Bn HQ started. 2 old Bosch shafts below firmed up.	
"	10th		As on 9th. HQ & 2 sections moved to HINDENBURG line in camp badly shelled during night of 9th/10th. Bivouacs thrown in but nobody injured.	
"	11th		As on 9th. 1 & 2 Corporal wounded by splinters from shell. Immediate wounded by Bn Norfolk platoon.	
"	12th		2 Sections on M.G. and Bn HQ dug outs. 2 Sections with 3 coys by on forward outposts during C.T.R.	
"	13th		Reinvoust. Moved of right sub forward to ROTTEN ROW with traverses through 3'6" deep, 4'6" dry.	
"	14th		As on 12th. Jumps dug in previous night deepened, sunk along front.	
"	15th		As on 12th. Heads of left traverse outposts found which traversed through & partially lined. One trench arranged of infantry. Work could not be completed.	
"	15th		Rest, cleaning kit & equipment. Rifle & gas helmet inspection.	
"	16th		Work on trench between left traverse outposts completed to 3'6" & wired. Very wet night.	

Army Form C. 2118.

WAR DIARY
INTELLIGENCE SUMMARY

79th Fld Co. R.E.

Place	Date	Hour	Summary of Events and Information	Remarks and references to Appendices
HENINEL	May 17th		Whole of new line completed to 3'6" deep and wired low wire. Carbon trench block in left dup and Dug out cont'd	
	18th		Three forward dups widened and deepened - work on tomb blocks for left and right dups and Dug outs cont'd	1 O.R. wounded by shell
	19th		Further work on dubs tomb blocks and Dug outs. 1 O.R. killed 1 died of wounds 4 wounded	
	20th		3 sections standing by for special work - 4th section continued on Dug outs. 1 O.R. wounded	
	21st		Relieved by and took over work of 92nd Fld Co. R.E. Wiring and digging on support line — new wiring at night	
	22nd		boring digging and carting on support line. Night work 2 shifts	
	23rd		" " " "	
	24th		" " " 3 Reinforcements arrived	
	25th		Wiring on support line. No working parties at night. Day Party cleaning up Concrete Trench.	
	26th		" " Digging Concrete Trench	
	27th		" " " Fair weather track Bridges req'd. Completed Repairs to Red Post at "The Rookery". Forming 4th forward Posts	
	28th		" " " and shovel Dump	
	29th		" " " Baby shelters for gunners . Working Parts digging Concrete trench at night. Started 2 Tunnel	
	30th		Shelters for D281 Bty. mined dugouts for D82 Bty. Dugouts for D82 Bty. Working party for Concrete trench cancelled. Day Party cleaning up Concrete Trench.	
	31st		O.C. returned from 10 day leave to England. As on 30th except working party not cancelled.	1 O.R. WEIR wounded by splinter

J. Sutter
Major R.E.
O.C. 79 Field Co. R.E.

WAR DIARY
INTELLIGENCE SUMMARY
(Erase heading not required.)

Army Form C. 2118.

JUNE

79th Field Coy R.E. Vol 24

Place	Date	Hour	Summary of Events and Information	Remarks and references to Appendices
HENIN EL	June 1st	—	Company on dug outs for Div. R.A. 1 attached platoon cleaning out CONCRETE Trench	2 GREEN 10 day leave to ENGLAND.
"	2nd	—	As on 1st except 2 more attached platoons on lining in front of CONCRETE TT.	
"	3rd	—	No 2nd	
"	4th	—	No 3rd	4 platoons Inf. working on CONCRETE TT
"	5th	—	No 4th up to 2 pm. 2 sections + attached platoons broke off 24 hrs off.	
"	6th	—	As on 5th 2 sections + attached platoons on the 2 who off. 2 sections inspected for hol els.	
"	7th	—	2 Sections inspected for hol els. By 2 pm. all sections on dug outs again. Work on dug outs for No 109 Battery + B/82 started. 6 platoons Inf. working on CONCRETE + BOTHAM TT in addition to 2 attached platoons lining + 1 attached platoon on firelays.	
"	8	—	Work on dug outs as before	
"	9	—	— do —	
"	10	—	— do —	Dug out in new sector started. Sector taken over by division 11/12
"	11	—	— do —	
"	12	—	— do —	1/2 company tratts
"	13	—	— do —	1/2 company tratts. Supervising Eng on SHAW/ST.
"	14	—	— do —	Attached platoons returned to battalions

Army Form C. 2118.

WAR DIARY
INTELLIGENCE SUMMARY
(Erase heading not required.)

79th Field Coy RE

Place	Date	Hour	Summary of Events and Information	Remarks and references to Appendices
	June			
HENINEL	15		Work on dug out.	
"	16		Handed over to 447th Field Coy RE	
"	17		Marched to SOUASTREE about 15 miles	
SOUASTREE	18		Settling in & cleaning up. Baths.	
"	19		Training	
"	20		Route march & training. Lt PICKERING joined Company	
"	21		Entrained at SAULTY LARBRET with 80th Field Coy RE. Trottingham left behind. Left 9.25pm	
YPRES	22		Detrained HOPOUTRE. Raining. Marched to DOMINION camp about 5 miles	
-do-	23		Moved camp to H13d62	
"	24		1 Section in Corps Workshops, remainder cleaning wagons etc	
"	25		Company training	
"	26		1 Section Corps Workshops. 3 Sections under Capt Knight moved to PIONEER Camp	
"	27		3 Sections started work on tracks, 1 Section in Corps Workshops	
"	28		As above. Kharty 150 bdg on night 27/28th	
"	29		3 Sections baths & inspection. 1 Section Corps Workshops. Capt Knight temporarily detached as OC 92nd Field Coy RE	
"	30		Work as on 27th. Lieut Hayden attached from 80th Field Coy RE	

Jn Sindler Capt
comm. 79th Field Coy RE
OC 79

WAR DIARY
INTELLIGENCE SUMMARY

Army Form C. 2118.

17

Vol 25

79th Field Coy RE

Place	Date	Hour	Summary of Events and Information	Remarks and references to Appendices
YPRES	July 1st		3 Sections on tracks. 1 Section Corps Workshops.	
"	2nd		As above except 1/2 Section tracks, inspection	
"	3rd		2 Sections on tracks. 1 1/2 Section tracks & inspection. 1/2 Section Corps Workshops. 1 Section on 105th field	
"	4th		1 Section on tracks, 100 Inf. 1 Section tracks inspection, 1 Section Corps Workshops. 1 Section with 105th field Coy RE on dug outs	
	5th		As on 4th	
	6th		As on 4th. Orders received to move to 30th Division Area at 10.30am ons 4th inst	
YPRES			Moved (except H.26.6.34.) Took our works of 200th Field Coy R.E.	
ZILLEBEKE	7th		2 Sections moved to ZILLEBEKE Bund in early morning. Remainder settled in Runnimeade Camp in MAPLETY CRESCENT. 2 Sections training, work in camp	
	8th		Work started on 3 Battalion H.Q. 50 Inf. Ranging parts. 2 Sections training work in camp	
	9th		As on 9th	
	10th		" "	
	11th		Reserve. E coy. a norfolk Platoon were attached for work	
	12th		2 Sections in ZILLEBEKE Bund on B° Hd. in Maple Ty. 1 Section work in camp	
	13th		Tin dumps. 1 section on ATN Park tracks	
	14th		As on 13th	
	15th		As on 14th	

Army Form C. 2118.

WAR DIARY
or
INTELLIGENCE SUMMARY. 79th Field Coy RE
(Erase heading not required.)

Instructions regarding War Diaries and Intelligence Summaries are contained in F. S. Regs., Part II. and the Staff Manual respectively. Title pages will be prepared in manuscript.

Place	Date	Hour	Summary of Events and Information	Remarks and references to Appendices
YPRES.	16th		Work as on 12th.	
			No 4 Section relieved No 7 Section in ZILLEBEKE Bund. Norfolk platoon moved to Bund	
ZILLEBEKE	17th		Work as on 12th. Lt Holmes rejoined company from 53rd Bde HQ. 1 Suffolk platoon attached for work	
"	18th		No 2 Section relieved No 3 Section. Work as before	
"	19th		Work as on 12th	
"	20		Work as on 12th	
"	21		Work as on 20th	
"	22		Work as on 21st	
"	23		Started to move camp to site near DICKEBUSH. Work as before	
DICKEBUSH	24		Finished moving camp. Work as before	
"	25		Work as before. No 2 & 4 Sections & Norfolk Platoon returned from the Bund.	
"	26		Rifle & Box respirator inspection. Baths. 1 Section work on dumps & tracks. Lt Hay dem returned Bo's Ludley	
"	27		Kit inspection + training. Baths. 1 Section work on dumps + tracks.	
"	28		Training. "W" day. Lt Leslie Smith Wounded by his horse coming down + turned it into a tent awhile	
"	29		Preparing for "Y" day. training. Berkshire platoon joined	
"	30		"Y" day. 4 Sections and Norfolk platoon marched to ZILLEBEKE Bund on 4/2 mgNC under orders D & 8th B & Norfolk R. O.C. reported at Brigade HQ. C.S.M. left in charge of camp + horselines	

Army Form C. 2118.

WAR DIARY
INTELLIGENCE SUMMARY.
79th Field Coy R.E.
(Erase heading not required.)

Place	Date	Hour	Summary of Events and Information	Remarks and references to Appendices
DICKE BUSH	July 31st		4 Sections + attached Platoons detailed for 4 S.P.s to man the Green line. Garrison to include 1 Norfolk platoon + 1 M.G. detachment in addition. Due to limited success of operations, these S.P.s were not required + orders to stop the parties on the way were sent. The garrison of S.P. "B" went off + went forward + dug themselves in in the front line + were relieved by the 30th Divs on the night of 30/31st July. 1st Army Arrangements from a R.E. company point of view were very unsatisfactory + a report of that effort was sent in on return. Sections were under orders of infantry numerous mistakes which should have been avoided were made. Rations had been ordered up on the assumption that the Green line was taken + as orders to stop the rations being sent up were not given in time, forks etc. rations right up to the front line. We lost 4 horses killed + 4 horses + mules wounded of which 2 were evacuated 2 done. Total casualties 2 Sergeants, 1 Corporal + 6 Sappers wounded. Corp S. wounded but still at duty. 3 Sections returned about 8 p.m. having got a lift down in an empty train. Remaining Section + Platoon returned the next morning July 31st at noon.	margin: 79 F.C. 79 [signed] Field 79th F.C.

Army Form C. 2118.

WAR DIARY
INTELLIGENCE SUMMARY.
(Erase heading not required.)

79th Field Coy RE

Vol 26

Place	Date	Hour	Summary of Events and Information	Remarks and references to Appendices
	August			
DICKEBUSH	1		Rest after 2 day. Rifle Inspection. Rain all day	
"	2		Rifle Inspection & box respirators. Physical training. Wet most of the day	
"	3		2 Sections moved to dugouts shelters in CHATEAU SEGARD area. Wet all day	
"	4		2 Sections on mule track to CASTLE STIRLING remainder work in camp	
"	5		2 Sections on mule track. 2 sections erecting NISSEN huts	
"	6		2 Sections on mule track. 2 Sections completing NISSEN huts & in tracks to ZILLEBEKE	
"	7		2 Sections on mule tracks. 2 section on tracks to ZILLEBEKE	
"	8		As on 7th tonight 2 sections from mule track to varying forward dumps	
"	9		Work in camp. Rifle & box respirator inspection	
"	10		Work in camp. tattlushe stations	
"	11		OC & 4 sections moved to ZILLEBEKE Bund	
"	12		OC & 2 officers went mud line. 2 section wing 2 posts by night advanced opening up C.T.S.	
"	13		Operations delayed 2 Sections wiring advanced posts by night	
"	14		2 Sections wiring right forward completed 300x	
"	15		Formed small forward dump with all available RE & Infantry	
"	16		2 sections tattleshe platoons (total 72 all ranks) left at Zero plus 15 mins, met I company of murphies on the way up to consolidate line stones points & others up to C.T.s leading letters	

T2134. Wt. W708—776. 500000. 4/15. Sir J. C. & S.

Army Form C. 2118.

WAR DIARY
or
INTELLIGENCE SUMMARY.

79ᵃ Field Coy R.E.

(Erase heading not required.)

Place	Date	Hour	Summary of Events and Information	Remarks and references to Appendices
	August			
DICKEBUSH	16	cont	Due to objective not being taken, 1 man stopped on the way up, 2 plates on sights about 7 hrs. received orders to return. 1 Section went up in the evening to warn 2 advanced posts & dig for boys.	
"	17		Company returned to whole line	
"	18		Left with our logs to rest Billets STEENVOORDE for the night Permission to march given us to return on train. 14 miles	
STEENVOORDE	19		Arrived LACLOCHE 12 noon 10 miles. Scattered billets	
LACLOCHE	20		2 Sections changed billets. Other two Sections. Rifle Inspection	
"	21		Baths & section training.	
"	22		Company training	
"	23		- do -	
"	24		- do -	
"	25		- do -	
"	26		Trip to seaside in lorries for 80 men for today	
"	27		Company training	
"	28		- do -	
"	29		- do -	
"	30		- do -	
"	31		Sports	

WAR DIARY or INTELLIGENCE SUMMARY

Army Form C. 2118.

79th Field Coy RE

WO1 27

Place	Date	Hour	Summary of Events and Information	Remarks and references to Appendices
LA CLOCHE	Sept: 1st		Carried out tests with Frank pattern "Bangalore Torpedoes" for 3rd Army.	
"	2nd		Church parade	
"	3		Company Training	
"	4th		Company training sports for divisions	
"	5 to 23rd		Company training includes work on storing huts, wiring drills & pontoons	
"	22nd		Warned for move but move cancelled on 22nd	
"	24		Company training	
"	25		- do -	
"	26		- do -	
"	27		Getting ready to move. It dawns to rest camp	
"	28		Dismounted by horse cylist & transport by road to YPRES area	
YPRES	29		Settling in & looking at new work (11th yearly to man at XVIII Corps School)	
"	30		Work started on slab road to ST JULIEN - POELCAPELLE road with RE.	
			Attached platoons formed 4 platoons & 2 officers total 122 all ranks	

JWS Lester
Major RE
79 Field Coy RE
oc 79

79TH FIELD COMPANY R.E. 2718.
Army Form No. Date 31/10/17

WAR DIARY
INTELLIGENCE SUMMARY. 79th Field Coy. R.E.
(Erase heading not required)

Place	Date	Hour	Summary of Events and Information	Remarks and references to Appendices
YPRES	October 1		Whole company on roads. '8' slab road 30' road bed	
"	2 & 3		As on 1st	
"	4		Half Coy employed only due to operations. 1/2 coy rest	
"	5		As on 1st	
"	6		As on 1st. Work delayed by rain & traffic	
"	7		As on 6th	
"	8		100 men 63rd Dis for work on road attached. Work delayed by 3hrs shelling	
"	9		As on 6th	
"	10		As on 9th. Tools and work of 67th Field Coy R.E.	
"	11		1 Section repairing bridge over R. LEKKERBOTERBEEK. 3 Sections within camp. Refit gas helmet	inspection
"	12		3 sections attached Platoons marched up at zero plus 1 1/2 hrs to a place of readiness but as the objectives were not taken returned to camp. Zero plus 8 hrs	
"	13		Work in camp	
"	14		3 sections roll called Platoon laying duckboards. 1 Section attached platoon work in camp	
"	15		1/2 Company laying duckboards. 1/2 coy work in camp	
"	16		1/2 Company laying duckboards. 1/2 work in forward camp	

Army Form C. 2118.

WAR DIARY
INTELLIGENCE SUMMARY
(Erase heading not required.)

79th Field Coy RE

Place	Date	Hour	Summary of Events and Information	Remarks and references to Appendices
YPRES	October 17th		1 Section attached platoon laying duckboards remainder work on forward camp	
"	18th		Attached Infants laying duckboards pushing up stores. Sections on forward camp	
"	19th		As on 18th	
"	20th		As on 19th	
"	21st		Work in camp. Baths.	
"	23rd		3 Sections & attached platoons left at 3am to take part in operations against POEL CAPELLE. Attached at RUOOLST+E FM for tea. No 3 Section attached platoon ordered at 7.45 am to move to PHEASANT FM. Nos 1+2 Sections + attached platoons left about 8am but later on 2 in command at Brigade HQ. OC went up to PHEASANT FM & started off all three sections. No 1 left HQ at 9 am & followed No 3 Section & attached platoon found they held HQ along them both sides of them along hot ratrutes. Their route lay up the fire beat & the old which was occupied by Hu & found nothing of the land on the way up. He left who held down nothing at the land on the way up. He left who held down nothing at No 3 Sections arranged with OC Northern found up some men of their party to the front in front of Arundy arrived by 6 at and did not complete the work required but got into no position it did not manage to get any of the party up. Very truly many wounded lost by hugust the OC 2 sections eventually been shared into brigade Hd.	

WAR DIARY or INTELLIGENCE SUMMARY

Army Form C. 2118.

79th Field Coy RE

(Erase heading not required.)

Place	Date	Hour	Summary of Events and Information	Remarks and references to Appendices
YPRES	22nd		Cont[inued] fg 36 horse watering trough. No Sections out.	
	23rd		3 Sections returned from instruction. No Sections out at camp.	
	24		Very wet ground. 1 N.C.O. 35 Other ranks wounded. 2 M.T. dvrs killed & N.C.O. & 1 Inf. wounded.	
	25		Working camp baths.	
	26		Moved 5,800 ton EN Camp, coast forward. Bombed at night, wounded 2 N.C.O. & 7 Sappers & drivers, & 2/4 Inf. & horses. Inf. wounded 1 died.	
	27		Settling in cleaning up. Inf. & Fd. Amb. buried this battalion. Transport rejoined HQ.	
	28		Work unmoved. Setting up. -do-	
	29		-do-	
	30		Marched to PROVEN area. Very wet march. Billets fair. Tired.	
	31		Drying & cleaning up.	On Dutch interview OC 79 joined 38 MC

WAR DIARY or INTELLIGENCE SUMMARY

Army Form C. 2118.

79th Field Co. R.E.

NOVEMBER

Place	Date	Hour	Summary of Events and Information	Remarks and references to Appendices
Pilgrims Bump	1-11-17		Training	
"	2-11-17		"	
"	3-11-17		"	
Aveluy Bump	4-11-17		Moving from Pilgrims Bump to Aveluy Bump via Ouppe Baleurst	
"	5-11-17		Making Bump	
"	6-11-17		1/2 of 3 Section & attached Platoon making & improving front Shelters	
"	7-11-17		do	1 h.C.O. wounded
"	8-11-17		3½ Section & attached Platoon	do
"	9-11-17		3½ " + ½ Inf Platoon making & improving front Shelters & solving Tracks leading to	1 Infantryman wounded
"	10-11-17		Aire Bump	
"	10-11-17		3½ Section + ½ Inf Platoon " " " "	1 Pte Looking from Rugby Dump
"	11-11-17		1 Section + attached Platoon " " " "	
"	"		½ " + " " " " moved to Montreuil farm to line, shelled out some night	
"	"		½ " + " " " " guides + putting material forward	O.C.: Major H Hadden, M.C., R.E. & 1 h.C.O. wounded.
"	12-11-17		2 Section + " making & improving shelters forward	
"	"		1/3 + " " moved to Becourt farm but shelled out & returned	

Army Form C. 2118.

WAR DIARY
or
INTELLIGENCE SUMMARY.
(Erase heading not required.)

November 1917.

Instructions regarding War Diaries and Intelligence Summaries are contained in F. S. Regs., Part II. and the Staff Manual respectively. Title pages will be prepared in manuscript.

Place	Date	Hour	Summary of Events and Information	Remarks and references to Appendices
Boesinghe	12-11-17		1/2 Section & attached Platoon wiring under 2/Lt Pickering. Daily practice to found Dumps	
"			1/2 " " " Guide & preparing material forward.	
"	13-11-17		2 Section " " Rest in camp & Boys sort	
"	14-11-17		2 " " " 1 Sapper & Pte Wounded. Wiring Posts & Drainage at Pascal Farm	
"	15-11-17		3.2 Sappers " " "	
"	16-11-17		All Sappers " " "	
"	17-11-17		Do " " "	
"	18-11-17		Do " " " 1 R.E.O wounded	
"	19-11-17		All " " "	
"	20-11-17		Taken over and relieved by 80th YMCA. Workin Bridgewood Atunbeck; Drainage and clearing of Atunbeck and Broenbeck Areas and preparing tarin Valleys, Stacking and Draining Canal Camp, Boesinghe Camp and Baboon Camp.	
	21		As above & Bridge over Atunbeck at Argus St.	
	22		As above	
	23		"	
	24		"	
	25		"	

Army Form C. 2118.

WAR DIARY
or
INTELLIGENCE SUMMARY.
(Erase heading not required.)

Instructions regarding War Diaries and Intelligence Summaries are contained in F. S. Regs., Part II. and the Staff Manual respectively. Title pages will be prepared in manuscript.

November 1917

Place	Date	Hour	Summary of Events and Information	Remarks and references to Appendices
Boesinghe	26		Works on Drainage and Bridges cont.d Preparing 500 yds of Camouflage screening with Postsand guys.	
	27		Works on Drainage and erection of Boesinghe Guard and Labor Camps cont.d 300 yds screening carried to Angle Point.	
	28		" " " " " " Bridges over Steenbeek at Railenstaad Aurgoett. 1 P.t.E. wounded	
	29		" " " " " " 300 yds screening carried to Alder Horse. 1 Soldr. killed 2 L/Cpls & Soldrs wounded.	
	30		Light Work. Camouflage screens erected ent vicinity of Angle Point and Alder Horse (14th Sherp Bdrs)	

R. S. Knight, Major, R.E.
O.C. 79th Field Coy. R.E.

DECEMBER.
79th Fd Coy RE
Vol 30

WAR DIARY
or
INTELLIGENCE SUMMARY.
(Erase heading not required.)

Army Form C2118.

Instructions regarding War Diaries and Intelligence Summaries are contained in F. S. Regs., Part II. and the Staff Manual respectively. Title pages will be prepared in manuscript.

Place	Date	Hour	Summary of Events and Information	Remarks and references to Appendices
Boesinghe	1-12-17		Easter Bros camouflage Screen at High Point & Alder House	
"	2-12-17		Inspection of huts & equipment. Military funeral. Baths.	
"	3-12-17		Nissen huts at Boesinghe Dump	
Plankbeek			Plankbeek Bridge & Railway Ft. Bridge completed	
XIX Corps area			Hutt Line, Wiring. Line completely reconstructed & marked	
"			Bunker Farm Drainage	
Bruno-Faxm 4-12-17			Drainage	
Hutt Line			Wiring material distributed along line to be wired 1700× to be done	
Boesinghe Dump 5-12-17			Billets. Accommodation for 3 Officers & 32 BOS. - Boring of Inundation.	
Hutt Line			Wiring. Double Apron. 2000×. 500× to complete	
Bruno Farm			Drainage	
Boesinghe Dump 6-12-17			Accom for Officers & ABOS course	
Hutt Line			Wiring. Double Apron 2500× complete	
Boesinghe Dump 7-12-17			Completion of Billets for attached Offr & ABO's	
Hutt Line			Wiring 450× of Double Bell Double Apron completed	
Bunker Farm			Drainage. Boy Haine Line De Wippe etc Improvements	

Army Form C. 2118.

WAR DIARY
or
INTELLIGENCE SUMMARY.
(Erase heading not required.)

Place	Date	Hour	Summary of Events and Information	Remarks and references to Appendices
Camp B6,2,5	3-12-17		Completed all existing huts with felt & wire netting.	
A 11 a 6.7			Improvements to Stables.	
Brower Farm			Drainage.	
Brower Farm	9-12-17			
Broodseinde			Drainage.	
Brower Farm	10-12-17		Drainage	
Broodseinde				
Bellevue Bump			Revetment of Specimen Nissen Hut.	
Bostinghe			Erecting to demolish Chateau Walls.	
A 11 a 6.7			Improvements to Stables.	
Support Line			Wiring. 800ˣ Double Apron wire complete. 1200ˣ	
Brower Farm	11-12-17			
A			Drainage.	
Broodseinde				
Bellevue Bump			Revetment Specimen Nissen Hut.	
Bostinghe Chateau			Demolition	
Support Line			Wiring. 1000ˣ of Double Double Apron complete. 1000ˣ to complete.	

Army Form C. 2118.

WAR DIARY
or
INTELLIGENCE SUMMARY.

(Erase heading not required.)

Instructions regarding War Diaries and Intelligence Summaries are contained in F. S. Regs., Part II. and the Staff Manual respectively. Title pages will be prepared in manuscript.

Place	Date	Hour	Summary of Events and Information	Remarks and references to Appendices
Brance farm & Busseboom	12-12-17		Drainage.	
Roberts Camp			Permanent Armun huts Hut completed.	
Boesinghe Chateau			Demolition completed	
Rupa Line			Wiring 1570' Double Double Apron completed. 500' to finish.	
Brance farm & Busseboom	13-12-17		Drainage.	
Rupa Line			Wiring 1700' Double Double Apron completed. 300' to complete.	
A11 a 6·7.			Improvements to Horse Lines.	
Brance farm & Busseboom	14·12·17		Drainage.	
A11 a 6·7.			Improvements to Horse Lines.	
Boesinghe camp			" to Drainage & revetting Huts	
Brance farm & Busseboom	15·12·17		Drainage.	
A11 a 6·7.			Improvements to Boy Horse Lines	

Army Form C. 2118.

WAR DIARY
or
INTELLIGENCE SUMMARY.
(Erase heading not required.)

DECEMBER

Instructions regarding War Diaries and Intelligence Summaries are contained in F. S. Regs., Part II. and the Staff Manual respectively. Title pages will be prepared in manuscript.

Place	Date	Hour	Summary of Events and Information	Remarks and references to Appendices
Bommezeele to Rousbrugge	16-12-17		Drainage.	
Rousbrugge				
Alla 6.7.			Coy Horse Lines. Improvement.	
Rousbrugge Camp			Improvements to Drainage & revetting	
	17-12-17		Moving Coy from Rousbrugge Camp to Elverdinghe Chateau	
Elverdinghe	18-12-17		Erecting Nissen Huts & Stables in vicinity of Elverdinghe	
"	19-12-17		" " " " " " "	
"	20-12-17		" " " " " " "	
"	21-12-17		" " " " " " "	
"	22-12-17		" " " " " " "	
"	23-12-17		Sunday. No Work. Rifle Inspection	
"	24-12-17		Erection Nissen Huts & Stables in vicinity of Elverdinghe	
"	25-12-17		Xmas Day. No work	
"	26-12-17		Erecting Nissen Huts & Stables in vicinity of Elverdinghe	
"	27-12-17		" " " " " " "	
"	28-12-17		" " " " " " "	

WAR DIARY
or
INTELLIGENCE SUMMARY.

(Erase heading not required.)

Army Form C. 2118.

DECEMBER

Place	Date	Hour	Summary of Events and Information	Remarks and references to Appendices
Elverdinghe	29-12-17		Furnishing Off jobs in vicinity of Elverdinghe	
"	30-12-17		Erecting Nissen huts in Elverdinghe Chateau garden	
"	31-12-17		"	

M.M. Moffatt
Capt.
79th. Field Coy.

Army Form C. 2118.

49th Div 6/18

WAR DIARY
or
INTELLIGENCE SUMMARY.   JANUARY.
(Erase heading not required.)

Vol 31

Place	Date	Hour	Summary of Events and Information	Remarks and references to Appendices
Boesinghe Camp	1-1-18		Moving Coy from Elverdinghe Chateau to Boesinghe Camp	
Elverdinghe Farm	2-1-18		Draining	
Elverdinghe	"		Erecting Huts Elverdinghe Chateau	
Boesinghe	"		Camp Improvement	
Elverdinghe Farm	3-1-18		Draining	
Bupa Line	"		Machine Gun Posts	
Koekuit Camp	"		Latrines & Collecting Material for Dump	
Elverdinghe	4-1-18		Drainage – Bupa Line M.G. Posts. Making Mean Road at Koekuit Dump	
Elverdinghe Farm	5-1-18		Drainage – Bupa Line M.G.	
"	6-1-18		" " " Boesinghe "	
"	7-1-18		" " " Moving Coy from Boesinghe Camp to Pascal Bend	
"	8-1-18		" " " Carrying out wiring Tapes on Bupa Line. Pascal Farm & VEE Bend	
"	"		" " " Making Man Road Boesinghe Dump	
Boesinghe Farm	9-1-18		" " " Erecting Wiring Material to Koekuit Dump	
"	10-1-18		" " "	
"	11-1-18		" " " – VEE Bend & Pascal Farm wiring	
VEE Bend Pascal Farm	12-1-18		Drainage for Shelter & erecting Shelter. Bupa Line completed wire VEE Bend & Pascal Farm wiring	
			Suffered killed. 8 Wounded. 1 attached Infantry Wounded	

Army Form C. 2118.

WAR DIARY
or
INTELLIGENCE SUMMARY.

(Erase heading not required.)

JANUARY.

Instructions regarding War Diaries and Intelligence Summaries are contained in F. S. Regs., Part II. and the Staff Manual respectively. Title pages will be prepared in manuscript.

Place	Date	Hour	Summary of Events and Information	Remarks and references to Appendices
Hondschoote	13-1-18		Repairing Bridges & Rolling Material to Kulient Dump.	
WEST hondschoote (huts)	14-1-18		Drawing & erecting shelter. V.E.E.Bend wiring Pascal farm wiring Eluidryke Chateau hutting	
"	15-1-18		" " " Pascal farm wiring Eluidryke Chateau building huts	
"	16-1-18		" " " " " "	
"	17-1-18		" " " " " "	
"	18-1-18		" " " " " "	
"	19-1-18		" " " " " "	
BUE SINGHE	20-1		Corps line wiring – Hutting Eluidrynghe Chateau	
	21-1		" " " "	
	22-1		" " " "	
	23-1		" " " "	
	24-1		" " " " Work handed over to 32nd Div'n	
Roudrughe Haringhe	25-1		Company moved by road to ROUSBRUGGE-HARINGHE Area (HAZEBROUCK Army)	
	26-1		Cleaning up hutments.	
	27-1		Company Training	
	28-1			
	29-1			
	30-1			
	31-1			

N.S. [illegible] Capt. F.
for O.C. 79th. Field Coy. R.E.

79th Coy R.E.

WAR DIARY
INTELLIGENCE SUMMARY. FEBRUARY.
(Erase heading not required.)

Vol 32

Place	Date	Hour	Summary of Events and Information	Remarks and references to Appendices
ROUSBRUGGE HARRINGHE	1, 2, 3, 4, 5, 6		Company training.	
			Preparation to move.	
			Company moved by Road and Rail to NOYON detrained and marched to BABŒUF (Map St QUENTIN)	
BABŒUF	7, 8			
"	9		Company moved by Road and horses to JUSSY (Map of front)	
BENAY	10		Noyard 4 sections moved to BENAY (" " ") Another Rhtt Zone for 3rd Corps	
"			"	
TERGNIGNY	26		Company relieved 89th Fd Co RE of 14th Div.	
	28		Work for 53rd Bde as required	

M Griffith Capt
Major, R.E.
O.C. 79th. Field Coy. R.E.

18th Div.

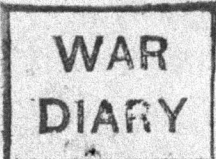

79th FIELD COMPANY, R.E.

MARCH

1918

WAR DIARY or **INTELLIGENCE SUMMARY**
(Erase heading not required.)

Army Form C. 2118

79/20 Coy R.E.
MARCH 1918

Place	Date	Hour	Summary of Events and Information	Remarks and references to Appendices
REMIGNY	1-3-18		2 Sections and attached Platoon at CAPONNE FARM. 2 Sections Hq and Horselines at REMIGNY.	
	20-3-18		Dispositions as above. Work for 53rd Bde on main line of Resistance from GUINGETTE FARM to MOY including Dugouts, Strong Points, wiring etc as required.	
LY-FONTAINE	21-3-18		Man Battle Positions	
RODEZ-WOOD	22		FRIERES-FAILLOUEL Men to man trenches in RODEZ WOOD	
CAILLOUEL	23rd		Rearguard action from RODEZ WOOD to CAILLOUEL to COMMENCHON including outpost duty night of 23rd.	
CAILLOUEL	24th		Dispositions as above. Battle positions in defensive line round CAILLOUEL	
VARESNES	25th		Retired to BABOEUF and then to VARESNES. Outpost duty at night N9015 E. CANAL; guarding bridges on PONTOISE-NOYON Road	
CAESNES	26th		Retired to CAESNES then marched to NAMPCEL.	
AUTRECHES	27th		Marched from NAMPCEL to AUTRECHES	
"	28th		Inspections drill etc at AUTRECHES	
"	29th			
	30th		By lorries to BOVES then marched to GENTELLES	
	31st		Wiring & digging on GENTELLES Defence Line	

B. Knight Maj RE
OC 79th Fld Coy RE.

18th Div.

79th FIELD COMPANY, R.E.

A P R I L

1 9 1 8

14

79 7th Coy R.E.

Army Form C. 2118

WAR DIARY
or
INTELLIGENCE SUMMARY
(Erase heading not required.)

APRIL Vol 34

Place	Date	Hour	Summary of Events and Information	Remarks and references to Appendices
GENTELLES	1st – 15th		Defensive works; digging, wiring etc on GENTELLES – CACHY – VILLERS – BRETONNEUX switch. Work for 53rd Bde as required. 2 officers killed in action 9.4.18.	
AMIENS.	13th – 26th		Marched to Billets at ECOLE NORMAL AMIENS. Horselines at SALOUEL. Company training. 4 Officers joined 23.4.18.	
WARLUS.	26th – 30th		Marched to WARLUS. Work as required for 53rd Bde and Company training.	

R S Kirwell Major, R.E.
O.C. 79th Field Coy. R.E.

WAR DIARY
or
INTELLIGENCE SUMMARY

Army Form C. 2118

MAY. 1918.

79th Field Coy R.E.

No 35

Place	Date	Hour	Summary of Events and Information	Remarks and references to Appendices
WARLUS Dieppe Map	1st 4th		Company training and improvements to 53rd Bde Area as required. Billets, Cookhouses, Latrines, Ablution benches etc.	
AGNICOURT Hinicourt Map	5th		Company moved by lorry from WARLUS to AGNICOURT. Transport moved by road to CONTAY.	
"	6th		Reconnaissance of Forward Area and site for forward camp.	
"	7th		2 Sections moved up and made Accom" for themselves at D.19.c.7.7.	
"	8th		H.Q. and remaining 2 Sections moved up & made Accom" at D.19.c.7.7 with Soland's Horse Arto & horses. Rail Pkt CONTAY.	
DIQc	9th		Reconnaissance of R.E. Bde. sector by all officers. Area straightening up Camp.	1 hm Wounded 17/5
	10th		2 Sections on Hewed dug outs; 1 Section on work for Bde Hq and Lumber supply; 1 Section on bivouacs.	- " - " 20/5
	↓		" " " " " " " " " " "	1 muck Killed 23/5/18
	24th		" " " " " " " " " " "	
Bois Robert	24th		Coy relieved by 1 Field Coy 47th Div. Horselines no change. Company moved to BOIS. ROBERT.	
	25th		Cleaning up; reconnaissance of BAISIEUX - WARLOY line.	
	26th ↓ 31st		Company moved to C.10.a. Horse lines no change. Company at work on above line with 55th Bde.	
			" " " "	
			" " " "	
			" " " "	

R.S. Knight
Major, R.E.
O.C. 79th Field Coy. R.E.

Army Form C. 2118.

WAR DIARY
or
INTELLIGENCE SUMMARY.
(Erase heading not required.)

79th Field Co R.E. Vol 36

JUNE 1918.

Place	Date	Hour	Summary of Events and Information	Remarks and references to Appendices
HENENCOURT WOOD.	1st		Company and Attached Platoons moved to Hevencourt Wood. Horselines no change remained at C.3.d.	
	2nd		Wiring, dugouts, Headquarters Accommodation for Observers as required by Brig. 53 and 54th Bdes.	
	"		"	
	15th		"	1 Sapper Killed — 2 O.R.s S⁄gts Wounded 5·6·18
	"		"	
	16th		Relieved in Left Brigade sector by 80th Field Co R.E. Billets and Horselines no change. Then Support Lineshaft	
			Work on Support line as required	
	26th		Relieved 80th Field Co R.E. in Left Bde sector. Billets and Horselines no change.	
	30th		Work as required in above sector.	

[signature]
Major R.E.
O.C. 79th Field Coy R.E.

WAR DIARY
or
INTELLIGENCE SUMMARY

(Erase heading not required.)

JULY – 1918 Army Form C. 2118.

79th Fld Coy R.E.

Vol 37

Place	Date	Hour	Summary of Events and Information	Remarks and references to Appendices
HENENCOURT WOOD	1st		Work for 5/A "K" Bde as required including Instruction for and training of Special Road Parties.	
	3rd		" " " "	
	4th		Work for 55th Bde as req'd	
	9th		" " " " " 2 Sappers joined 5.7.18	
	10th		" " " " Capt. Gourlay R.E. takes over command of Company ROUEN	
	11th		" " " " Major R.S. Knight R.E. struck off strength on leaving for Rouen	
			Work for 55th Bde	
	12th		Billeting & Transport leaves for rest area. Remainder of personnel embus at CONTAY	
LA CHAUSSÉE-TIRANCOURT	13th		6 p.m. arrive LA CHAUSSÉE – TIRANCOURT 9.45 p.m. Billets for whole coy.	
	14th		Pontoons trestle wagons arrive. Work on billets	
	15th		Church parade + work on billets	
			Training. Transport overhauled. 2 Sappers + 3 Drivers joined 19.7.18.	
	29		Various work parties; camps for Infantry + sports grounds	
	30		Loading portions of 3 Coys. Preparations for move into the Line. Advance party ¼ I.T. Haines to FRANVILLERS at noon.	
	31		Embus 12 noon. Arr. FRANVILLERS 5.20 p.m. Bivouacs – taken over from 81st Fd Coy. Petroleum Engineer. Pontoons sent to + dumped at VILLERS-BOCAGE	

K Gourlay. Major R.E.
O.C. 79th Field Coy. R.E.

18th DIVISION,
ENGINEERS

79th FIELD COMPANY R.E.

AUGUST 1918

79 Fd Coy RE

WAR DIARY or INTELLIGENCE SUMMARY

Army Form C. 2118.

AUGUST 1918.

WO/95/38

79TH FIELD COMPANY, R.E.
No. T.189
Date 31/8/18

Place	Date	Hour	Summary of Events and Information	Remarks and references to Appendices
FRANVILLERS	1st		Coy in Reserve. Work on Billets & reconnaissance of area.	
	2nd		'Inf' Pns & 'Lt OVENDEN & 'Lt ROBERTSON joined.	
	3rd 4		Work on 5ro Causeways wire. Billets work for attacking Pns. Work in preparation for attack.	
	5		Capt GREEN returned from PARIS leave. 'Lt YOUNG returned from T. School ROUEN.	
	567		Work on Adv Bde Hqrs for 53 Bde. No 4 Section selected & billetted forward.	
	7		Form section (O.C. 'Lt Mackay 'Lt Knight Harvie Young) in readiness to advance by 12 midnight.	
	89		Work on chains & roadbelts, strong points behind front of infantry advance. Funnel Section returned to lines 7 pm 9th.	
	10		Rest. Coy moved to HENENCOURT WOOD at 9 pm. Taken over from 517 Coy 47 Div.	
HENENCOURT	11		Taken over billets & work.	
	12 13		Work with 53 Bde on Coy & Bn Shelters. Reconnaissance of various localities & for material.	
	14-21		Work on field cration on ALBERT. AMIENS road. Want cutting. Various work for 53 Bde.	
DERNANCOURT	22nd		Coy attd to 53 Bde acts as Adv. Guard to Div. Section moved off 8 am to DERNANCOURT. Coy Hqrs left at HENENCOURT. Horse Lines moved from CONTAY to HENENCOURT.	
	23rd		Sections worked afternoon & evening on consolidation of 2nd line of defence E of ALBERT. & Slept at HENENCOURT BILLETS	

Army Form C. 2118.

WAR DIARY
or
INTELLIGENCE SUMMARY. AUGUST (cont)
(Erase heading not required.)

Place	Date	Hour	Summary of Events and Information	Remarks and references to Appendices
ALBERT	24th		Coy rested at HENENCOURT BILLETS	
	25.		Coy moved to bivouacs in railway embankment S. of ALBERT. Reconnaissance	
			made for 53 Bde. Trestle bridge demolished ALBERT. Trestle Bridge erected clear of roadway near VIVIER MILL ALBERT.	
	26th		2 Sections moved to BECOURT Wood on Div. H.Q. H & Y on roads	
MAMETZ	27		Remainder of coy moved to MAMETZ WOOD. R.E. Reconnaissance of forward areas & 53 Bde work	
	28		Windlass wells & pumping engines. 2 Sections for BECOURT power Coy.	
	29		Relocation of shelled hutments.	
TRONES WOOD	30		Coy moved 7.30 a.m. there were moved to MAMETZ WOOD. Work on troughs & steam pumping plant.	
	31		Water Supply works. Work on Artillery Hutments & Baths.	

M Gunlay Major, R.E.
O.C. 79th. Field Coy. R.E.

Appendix to War Diary for August. — **Reinforcements:-**

3 OR's joined on 17.8.18
6 OR's — . —   on 26.8.18.

Casualties
1 Pte (attached Essex Platoon) Wounded 8/8/18.

	79TH FIELD COMPANY, R.E.
	No. T.88.
	Date 31.8.18.

M Gourlay .... Major, R.E.
O.C. 79th. Field Coy. R.E.

WAR DIARY
or
INTELLIGENCE SUMMARY

79th Field Coy R.E.

SEPTEMBER 1918.

Vol 40

Place	Date	Hour	Summary of Events and Information	Remarks and references to Appendices
TRONES WOOD.	1st		Work on Wells, pumps & Baths Trones Wood Area.	
COMBLES	2nd		Nos 1 3 & 4 Sections moved to vicinity of COMBLES. Work on advance of 53 Bde R.E. Reconnaissance & preparation of Hrqrs for Brigades & Bns. Horse lines	
	3rd		Moved to TRONES WOOD	
			Preparations to bridge Canal du Nord & Tortille River. All Bridges equipment collected & put under disposal of Adv. Guard Coy. (79th Coy.) No 4 Section found R.E. Reconnaissance. 1 3 4 Section night at St PIERRE VAAST WOOD. No 2 Section moved to COMBLES also Horse Lines. Wood next RFA & Bde & on Transport Bridge near CANAL DU NORD.	
	4th		1 3 4 Section returned to COMBLES for night. Work as on 3rd.	
FAVIER WOOD	5th		Coy proceeded to Rob Billety by march route	
	6-15		Rest. Overhaul of equipment. Odd men working with Infantry. Parade ground made by filling shell holes.	
	10-15		Malaria. O.C. at Dr Hzn as O/Cer.	
	15		No 2 Section moves to LIERAMONT with an Adv. Bde Hqrs.	
NURLU	16		Coy moves to vicinity of Epinette wood where it bivouacs for the night. Horse Transport remains at MOISLAINS	

Army Form C. 2118.

WAR DIARY
or
INTELLIGENCE SUMMARY.
(Erase heading not required.)

Instructions regarding War Diaries and Intelligence Summaries are contained in F. S. Regs., Part II. and the Staff Manual respectively. Title pages will be prepared in manuscript.

Place	Date	Hour	Summary of Events and Information	Remarks and references to Appendices
SAULCOURT	17th		Coy joins No 2 Section. Horse Transport moves to LIERAMONT	
	18		Coy in Div Reserve for work of necessary w/k CRA. 1st Section working on waterpoints	
ST EMILIE	19		2,3,4 Section move up forward. Horselines move to vicinity of SAULCOURT	
	20		Odd work for Bde on taking over line	
	21		2,3,4 Section moved up to Line. Prepared to consolidate. 2 Section allotted to 1 Bde
			for Consolidation. One Section working on Div Line. Objective not gained. Section	
			returned to Lines evening.	
	22		Various small jobs for Bde. Standing by in billets for consolidation work	
	23		"700" Line taped for Pioneers to dig CT on. Bivouacked	
	24		Handed over to 27 Div. U.S. Engineers. Showed them around Line &c.	
MAUREPAS	25		Coy moved by march route to ROUGE FERME. Billets	
	26-27		Rest. Coy paraded w/t 53 Bde to hear address from Div Commander.	
SAULCOURT	28		Coy marched by bus to Line. Transport arrived at new billets 8 p.m. Horse	
			Lines near LIERAMONT	
	29		Section moved forward w/t attended numbers formed to work on Canal Crossings	
			w/t ST QUENTIN CANAL at VENDUILE. Reconnaissance parties forward from	
			No 2 Section.	

Army Form C. 2118.

WAR DIARY
or
INTELLIGENCE SUMMARY.
(Erase heading not required.)

Instructions regarding War Diaries and Intelligence Summaries are contained in F. S. Regs., Part II. and the Staff Manual respectively. Title pages will be prepared in manuscript.

Place	Date	Hour	Summary of Events and Information	Remarks and references to Appendices
SAULCOURT	30		Section moved forward from Villers again in reports of infantry entry	
			VENDHUILE Reconnaissance made of bridges Yench etc Preparation made to bring up stores to repair H.T. Bridges. No work done to enemy commanded canal still.	

K P Gourlay
Major, R.E.
O.C. 79th. Field Coy. R.E.

79th Field Co. Royal Engineers

Nominal Roll of N.C.O's & men taken on & struck of Strength during September.

	On Strength				Off Strength		
Reg No	Rank	Name	Date	Reg No	Rank	Name	Date
65393	Spr	Newman S.F.	7/9/18	170941	Spr	Stirrup J.	4.9.18
245327	Pnr	McGuire W.	7/9/18	52145	Sgt	Worsley J.H.	2.9.18
51252	Sjt	Whitehead A.		199176	2Cpl	Steele W.	11.9.18
176625	"	Galbraith W.		61822	Spr	Williams F.	2.9.18
186424	"	Whitehead H.	15/9/18	186032	2Cpl	Jones R.	22.9.18
82801	"	Mann F.	15/9/18	104419	L"	Ward M.J.	22.9.18
134049	"	Eldridge W.		46319	Cpl	Kent J.W.(MM)	22.9.18
80558	2Cpl	Pattyson J.		512144	Spr	Williams W.	22.9.18
236475	Spr	Noble H.		360538	"	Hartung W.	30.9.18
160264	"	Robinson G.W.	27/9/18	454718	"	Mowbray G.	28.9.18
278319	"	Stadcroft B.	27/9/18	426404	"	Stuart J.	28.9.18
186269	"	Green E.G.		440193	"	Reynolds C.	29.9.18
96404	"	Thatcher A.(MM)		176765	"	Kersley C.	28.9.18
522283	"	Tomlin H.					

K.Gourlay
Major R.E.
O.C. 79th. Field Coy. R.E.

Army Form C. 2118.

WAR DIARY
or
INTELLIGENCE SUMMARY.
(Erase heading not required.)

OCTOBER 1918
79 Fn Coy R.E.
Vol 40

Instructions regarding War Diaries and Intelligence Summaries are contained in F.S. Regs., Part II. and the Staff Manual respectively. Title pages will be prepared in manuscript.

Place	Date	Hour	Summary of Events and Information	Remarks and references to Appendices
SADLCOURT	1		Relief by 50th Div. Transport to Caterpillar Valley (MAMETZ).	
BEAUCOURT	2		Men entrained 1000. Moved to BEAUCOURT. Transport joined Coy	
"	3-15		Rest. Manu work. Afternoons chiefly devoted to sports &c.	
"	16		Transport to Caterpillar Valley leaves 1700.	
AMIENS	17		Men marched to POULAINVILLE entrained 1400. Arrived ROISEL at 0100 approx.	
VILLERS FAUCON			Transport joined at VILLERS FAUCON	
PREMONT	18		entrained there. arrived 1700. Billets. Transport by road.	
"	19-20		Billets.	
MAUROIS	21		Coy moved complete arriv 1100.	
"	22		Wagon loaded with outfits, Bridges & 3 Spans 15' sent up to le CATEAU	
LE CATEAU	23		1400 Hrs Coy made 4 crossings for Artillery over RICHEMONT Stream. Laid tape lines Forward Reconnaissance.	
	24		1100 Horse lines joined Coy. Reconnaissance continued. Water Tanks & troughs laid	
	25-31		w/c done on baths at le CATEAU.	
	31		2 Sections working at Renvort Farm. O.C. on hospitable sick	

E.T. Green
Major R.E.
O.C. 79th. Field Coy. R.E.

NOVEMBER 1918   Army Form C. 2118.

79 Fd Coy R.E.

Vol 41

WAR DIARY
or
INTELLIGENCE SUMMARY.
(Erase heading not required.)

Place	Date	Hour	Summary of Events and Information	Remarks and references to Appendices
Le Cateau	1-2		Work on Louviarie baths & Dump	
"	3		Company moved to Croix	
Croix	4		Section moved to H.E.Cg. repairing bridges & roads	
"			Transferred from Le Cateau to Croix.	
H.E.Cg	5		H.Q & transport to H.E.Cg. work road St Benin	
"	6		at H.E.Cg. work roads & repair	
"	7		Company moved to Maroilles	
Maroilles	8		work on bridge (C.25.d.3.8.)	
"	9-17		work on bridge (")	
Maurois	18		move to Maurois (Company in huts) Transport by march route	
Serain	19		" " Serain by march route	
	20		Salvage work. (Company hutted at Elincourt)	
	21-30		(1) Work at Beaurevoir, Ponchaux, & Premont (improvement of billets)	
			(2) Demolition party working in this area (destroying booby traps, land grenades, + bombs)	

E.T.Geen Capt R.E.
For O.C. 79th. Field Coy. R.E.

DECEMBER 1918. Army Form C. 2118.

79th Coy R.E.

WAR DIARY
or
INTELLIGENCE SUMMARY.
(Erase heading not required.)

Instructions regarding War Diaries and Intelligence Summaries are contained in F. S. Regs., Part II. and the Staff Manual respectively. Title pages will be prepared in manuscript.

Place	Date	Hour	Summary of Events and Information	Remarks and references to Appendices
SERAIN	1 to 22		& PREMONT AREAS Work at BEAUREVOIR, improvement of billets, destroying dud shells, hand grenades & bombs.	
-,-	23 to 26		Christmas break.	
-,-	27 to 31		Work on billets, recreation rooms etc. Demolition in 53rd Bde Area	

Fowler... Major, R.E.
O.C. 79th. Field Coy. R.E.

79TH Fld C.R.E.

WAR DIARY
or
INTELLIGENCE SUMMARY

Army Form C. 2118

JANUARY 1915 Vol 43

Place	Date	Hour	Summary of Events and Information	Remarks and references to Appendices
SERAIN	1/9 – 22/9		Work in Beauvoir & Fresnoy Areas, improvement of billets, destroying "Dud" shells, grenades, etc.	
CLARY	23/9 – 31/9		Various work to be done in CLARY & BERTRY Sectors - Repairs billets	

Signature, Major
O.C. 79th. Field Coy. R.E.

WAR DIARY
or
INTELLIGENCE SUMMARY.

79th Fd Coy R.E. Army Form C. 2118.

Place	Date	Hour	Summary of Events and Information	Remarks and references to Appendices
CLARY	1-28 Feb.		Coy. demobilising to "B" Cadre. Work on Inf'y Billets. fixing 9 tennis & E.L. sets. Clearance of wells for Civil authorities	

Major,
O.C. 79th. Field Coy. R.E.

WAR DIARY
or
INTELLIGENCE SUMMARY.
(Erase heading not required.)

179 Field Coy. R.E.

MARCH 1919.   Vol. 1 & 5

Army Form C. 2118.

Place	Date	Hour	Summary of Events and Information	Remarks and references to Appendices
CLARY	1/3/19 18/3/19		Coy. Demolished down to A Sector. — Storing & repairing lighting sets	
CAUDRY	19/3/19 31/3/19		Repairing of French Houses occupied as billets.	

[signature] Capt. R.E.
179th. Field Coy. R.E.

WAR DIARY
or
INTELLIGENCE SUMMARY.

(Erase heading not required.)

49th Division R.E. April 1919.

Army Form C. 2118.

Place	Date	Hour	Summary of Events and Information	Remarks and references to Appendices
Calais	1/4 to 30/4		Cleaning & oiling of Transport. Checking & Closing of Stores.	N.R.

www.ingramcontent.com/pod-product-compliance
Lightning Source LLC
Chambersburg PA
CBHW081427160426
43193CB00013B/2211